From a Traditional Greek Kitchen

Vegetarian Cuisine

by Aphrodite Polemis

The Book Publishing Company
Summertown, Tennessee

Published in the US by
Book Publishing Company
PO Box 99
Summertown, TN 38483
(888) 260-8458

Cover and interior design by Barbara McNew
Cover photography by John Guider
Food Stylist for cover, Mary Ann Fowlkes

ISBN13 978-0-913990-93-3   ISBN10 0-913990-93-0

12 11 10 09 08   3 4 5 6 7 8

Printed in Canada

Library of Congress Cataloging-in-Publication Data
Polemis, Aphrodite.
       From a traditional Greek Kitchen/ Aphrodite Polemis.
              p. cm
       Includes index
       ISBN0-913990-93-0
       1. Vegetarian Cookery. 2. Cookery, Greek I. Title
       TX837.P65 1992
       641.5945-dc20   92-18500
                     CIP

Calculations for the nutritional analyses in this book are based on the average number of servings listed with the recipes and the average amount of an ingredient if a range is called for. Calculations are rounded up to the nearest gram. If two options for an ingredient are listed, the first one is used. Not included are fat used for frying, unless the amount is specified in the recipe, optional ingredients, or servings suggestions.

Book Publishing Co. is a member of Green Press Initiative. We chose to print this title on paper with postconsumer recycled content, processed without chlorine, which saved the following natural resources:

 green press INITIATIVE

618 pounds of solid waste   4,813gallons of water
1,159 pounds of greenhouse gases   13 trees
             9 million BTU of energy

For more information, visit <www.greenpressinitiative.org>. Savings calculations thanks to the Environmental Defense Paper Calculator, <www.papercalculator.org>.

Table of Contents

Introduction

I compiled these recipes for people who not only love good food, but are also interested in good health and want to try a unique cuisine.

Nowadays, it seems almost impossible to find a true vegetarian recipe in Greek cuisine because meat and fish are added to so many dishes. This was not always the case. In the past meat was reserved almost exclusively for Christmas, the local Saints' days and Easter, especially for the poor Greek families.

With this book I'm reviving the old days with genuine Greek recipes, as well as flavorful vegetarian versions of other traditional dishes. In some cases meatless dishes have been modified to be more in line with today's health consciousness. For instance, in the age-old meat and macaroni dish, *Pastitsio*, I successfully substituted chick peas for chopped meat and eliminated eggs in the sauce by adding more cheese.

I did not write this book only for the experienced vegetarian, but for anyone who knows a vegetarian diet will benefit them and is worried that vegetarian food must be boring. Let me show you that being a vegetarian does not mean living on lettuce and carrots! Feel free to experiment with different recipes to suit your own eating style. Step into Aphrodite's Vegetarian Kitchen, and discover a new, delicious and healthful eating experience.

Kali Orexi!

About Greek Ingredients

Feta

Feta is the Greek cheese best known by Americans and is the most popular native cheese in Greece. Soft and very salty, it is usually made from goat's milk. Sometimes sheep's milk is mixed in which makes the cheese taste less sharp. The Greeks believe that a piece of feta eaten before the fruit course helps digest the meal. Feta is also served during the meal, particularly if the main course is a vegetable. You can substitute dry cottage cheese, farmer's cheese or ricotta, but the result will not be the same; feta is worth looking for.

Mizithra, kefalotyri, and kasseri cheeses

Mizithra is a mild sheep's milk cheese, delicious in Honey Cheese Cake (pg. 174). Kefalotyri, a hard sheep's milk cheese, is used for grating onto pasta; you can substitute parmesan for it. Kasseri was introduced to the Greeks by the Italians, who most likely got it from the Bulgarians. It is made from a mixture of goat's and sheep's milk. Quickly fried, it makes a wonderful first course call *Saghanaki* (pg. 17).

Tahini

Tahini is a thick puree of sesame seeds. It has a nutty flavor and can be found in many grocery and specialty stores. When a recipe calls for tahini, there can be no substitute.

Mahlepi

Mahlepi, a Turkish spice, is another ingredient for which there is no substitute. The exotic flavor and aroma it adds to *Easter Twists* (pg. 151) and *No-Yeast St. Basil's Cake* (pg. 154) is impossible to describe. Whole mahlepi seeds and powder are sold in Syrian or Greek stores. If only the seeds are available you can either pound them in a mortar to make a powder or boil one tablespoon in ⅓ cup water for 2 minutes, discard the seeds and substitute the liquid for 1 tablespoon of powder.

Orzo

Orzo is a tiny form of pasta about the same size as rice. It is also available at Greek food stores, or you may substitute a more conventional small pasta, if you are unable to obtain orzo.

Phyllo

Phyllo (pronouced Fee-lo) is a strudel dough made of just two ingredients: flour and water. In Greek the word "phyllo" means both a leaf and a page in a book. Phyllo strudel sheets are even thinner than the pages of this book. They are difficult to make at home but fortunately are sold in one pound packages at Greek grocery stores and many supermarkets. If the recipe you select calls for just ½ pound of phyllo, wrap the unused half very carefully in waxed paper and refrigerate; it keeps for 3 to 4 weeks.

Phyllo dries out rapidly when exposed to the air. In some recipes, like *Cheese Puffs* (pgs. 15 & 16), you'll be taking 6 to 7 sheets out of the package at one time, cutting them into strips and working with only a few strips at a time. Cover the strips you aren't going to use for a while with waxed paper and a damp (not wet) towel. Each sheet of phyllo should be brushed with melted butter or oil as you use it. This is essential to make the finished dish crisp and flaky, but you can use either one sparingly, brushing lightly, to reduce the amount of fat in the recipe.

Kataifi

Kataifi is another form of phyllo dough, which is shredded and packed in bags. When you are ready to use it place the shredded dough on a flat surface and loosen the strands with your fingers by gently shaking large handfuls of the dough.

Herb and Spice Glossary

Herbs and spices are to cooking what accessories are to clothing. A recipe may be fine by itself, but add a little garlic here or a little thyme there and you really have a dish worth savoring.

Almost everyone has some herbs and spices in the house. Below I describe which herbs are traditionally used in certain dishes, but I urge you to look through your cupboard and experiment with different herbs in your own preparations. Remember, however, that a little goes a long way; flavorings should complement a meal, not overwhelm it.

Herbs and spices do not only add zest to a meal. For thousands of years herbs have been used for their therapeutic qualities. Because this book of vegetarian recipes is for the health-conscious as well as the flavor-conscious, I wanted to include which herbs relieve which ailments.

While you should always seek a qualified medical opinion for a serious complaint, you can avoid drugs and relieve many minor, as well as major, ailments by using the right herbs.

When an herb is used for therapeutic reasons add a teaspoon to one cup of boiled water and let it steep for 3 to 5 minutes. Strain, serve with a few drops of lemon juice and honey, and reap the benefits of nature.

Chamomile
Chamomile tea is known as an aid for upset stomach, a tonic infusion and a calmant for the nerves.

Cinnamon
By boiling 2 sticks of cinnamon and drinking the water, cinnamon is beneficial as an antiseptic, a disinfectant and a cleanser of infections of the urinary tract.

Cinnamon is well known as an aromatic spice for sweet dishes. I do not only use this spice in sweets but add it as a "secret" ingredient to sautéed vegetables such as eggplant and mushrooms.

Cloves

Medically, cloves regulate the activities of the brain, help neuralgia and stop pain, especially headaches and toothaches. An old remedy for toothache relief involves placing a piece of cotton saturated in clove oil on the aching tooth. This eases the pain until a dentist can be reached.

Cloves, like cinnamon, are also known for the aroma they add to sweets.

Dill

Dill contains two essential oils, limonese and carvone, which make it valuable as a digestive aid. It is also considered to be a good cure for hiccoughs and insomnia.

As an ingredient dill is delicious with artichokes, peas and spinach. It is also tasty sprinkled on boiled potatoes and potato salad.

Garlic

The Greek villagers used to say "Don't let a day pass without eating garlic." As well as being delicious it really is an amazing medicine. Garlic contains an essential oil known as allyl sulphide. Its pungent smell comes from the sulphur.

Garlic comes in handy as an antiseptic, a cough medicine and a stimulant. It is also said to help circulation and is therefore prescribed in powder form by some herbalists as a brain developer. To lower blood pressure it is recommended that you leave a minced clove of garlic overnight in a glass of water and drinking the water in the morning.

Garlic is used in almost all the stew and sauce recipes in this book. Try using it in soups and salads as well.

Laurel (Bay Leaf)

The ancient Greeks crowned their heroes with wreaths of laurel leaves. The ancient Romans believed it protected them from lightning, thus prompting Julius Caesar to always sport a laurel wreath. You may not use laurel to protect yourself from bad weather or to denote your heroism, but you can use it to aid your rheumatism. Boil the leaves and flowers for 20 minutes, strain, add a lemon peel and drink a glass three times a day.

In cooking, laurel or bay leaves add a special aroma to stews and soups, especially *Stifatho* (Onion Stew, pg. 123) and lentil dishes.

Leeks

Leeks contain vitamins B and C, calcium, phosphorous, potassium, iron, magnesium and other nutrients. The ancients believed that leeks helped develop a deep, clear voice in men and fertility in women. By washing their noses with leek juice, nosebleeds were prevented.

I include leek as an herb as I included garlic. Leeks add a wonderful taste to stews, rice and soups.

Lemons

Lemons are the most valuable of fruits, full of vitamin C, iodine, phosphorus, iron and other nutrients. A preparation of one glass of water, the juice of one lemon and a little honey is not only a nice breakfast drink, but also beneficial for ailments of the kidneys, arthritis, diabetes and heartburn. A tablespoon of lemon juice and honey is famous for soothing a sour throat.

Lemon juice and lemon peel can be used with herbs in cooking. By adding a little lemon to your salad you can avoid using a more fattening dressing and cut the calories.

Marjoram

Marjoram contains oils that are both a stimulant and a tonic. It works wonders to relieve an upset stomach.

Parsley

Parsley has a high content of vitamins A, B, C and E. It is also loaded with iron, making it a healthy addition to any dish.

Parsley can be added virtually to any dish to add a fresh, herby flavor. Blending nicely with other herbs, except sage, it can be used in all stews, soups, salads and as a garnish.

Peppermint

Peppermint contains menthol oil. This makes peppermint tea an excellent aid for upset stomach, frayed nerves and colds.

Rosemary

Rosemary is a versatile and fragrant herb. It is known as a tonic, stimulant and antidepressive, and can relieve tension headaches.

In cooking, rosemary is usually used in stews and stuffed vegetables.

Sage

Sage is known to relieve nervous headaches and bleeding gums. It is also wonderful in relieving upset stomachs and menstrual pains.

Spearmint

Spearmint is a stimulant known for its antispasmodic properties and as an aid in digestion. Because of this it is useful in fighting nausea and vomiting. As a tea it is soothing to symptoms of colds or flu.

Thyme

Thyme contains invaluable oils and is known as an antiseptic as well as a digestive. Headaches, sore throats and coughs can be relieved from this aromatic herb.

In cooking, thyme is delicious in stews and stuffed vegetables.

Clarfied Butter

It is very helpful to use clarified butter when you are frying or sautéing. Clarifying prevents the butter from burning. I also use it when making baklava, to give it a rosy color that's not dark. Cut butter into chunks and melt it over low heat, being careful not to let it brown. Remove from heat and let stand 5 minutes. With a brush, remove all the froth from the surface. Then spoon off the clear butter and discard the milky solids at the bottom of the pan.

If you remove the froth and refrigerate the butter, it will be easier to separate the clear butter from the milky solids.

Appetizers

To make Baked Cheese Puffs triangles
Phyllo sheets strips 3½" x 12"

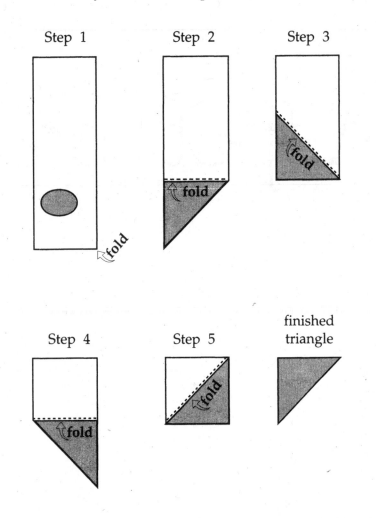

Step 1

Step 2

Step 3

Step 4

Step 5

finished triangle

Baked Cheese Puffs
Bourekakia
Makes 30 to 35 puffs

Bourekakia are delicious, and are more likely to be served in homes than in restaurants because they need to be made fresh and served hot.

See photo on front cover.

Mix cheeses and tofu (if used), egg, parsley and bread crumbs.

Take half the phyllo sheets from the package; place the rest in the refrigerator. Cut sheets into strips about 3½" x 12". Use 2 strips at a time, covering the remaining strips with waxed paper to prevent them from drying out.

Brush 1 strip lightly with melted butter, place the second strip on top and brush lightly again. Place 1 Tbsp. cheese mixture at one end of the layered strip. Lift a corner of the strip next to the filling and fold it over the filling so that it touches the opposite long side and forms a triangle enclosing the filling. Continue to fold up the pastry, maintaining the triangular shape. Fill and fold the remaining strips. Take the remaining phyllo sheets from the refrigerator and cut them into strips. Repeat the filling and folding process. Place the puffs in an oiled baking pan and brush lightly with melted butter. Bake in a preheated 350° oven until golden, about 20 minutes. If all the puffs do not fit into your baking pan, it is alright to let the extras wait until the first batch is baked; then use the same pan to bake the rest. Do not use baking sheets without sides because butter may drip out into your oven.

Note: *Baked Cheese Puffs may be frozen before baking; they will keep in the freezer for about 4 weeks. Stack upright in a freezer-proof container. To heat and serve, brush frozen puffs with melted butter and bake in a preheated 350° oven until golden, about 30 minutes.*

Per Puff: Calories: 58, Protein: 2 gm., Carbohydrates: 5 gm.

¼ lb. feta cheese, crumbled, or ¼ lb. tofu, crumbled, with 1 Tbsp. miso

¼ lb. ricotta cheese

1 large egg, lightly beaten, or egg substitute

1½ tsps. fresh parsley, finely chopped

1½ tsps. bread crumbs

½ lb. phyllo pastry

6 Tbsps. butter, melted

Fried Cheese Puffs
Bourekakia Tyghanita

Makes 30 to 35 puffs

½ lb. feta cheese,
  crumbled,
  or ¼ lb. feta and
  ¼ lb. ricotta,
  cream or farmer's
  cheese

¼ cup kefalotyri
  or parmesan
  cheese, grated

1 large egg, lightly
  beaten,
  or egg substitute

1 Tbsp. parsley, fine-
  ly chopped

½ lb. phyllo pastry

¼ cup olive oil
  or vegetable oil
  (for brushing)

Mix cheeses, egg and parsley.

Cut, fill and fold phyllo pastry as in *Baked Cheese Puffs*, page 15, except brush strips with oil. Heat 4 inches of oil in a deep-fryer to 350°.

Fry puffs until golden.

Per Puff: Calories: 63, Protein: 3 gm., Fat: 4 gm.,
  Carbohydrates: 5 gm.

Baked Cheese Sticks
Tyri Tou Fournou
Serves 4

Brush the bottom of a heatproof baking dish with olive oil. Slice cheese into 8 thick sticks and place on top of olive oil. Bake in a preheated 450° oven until cheese is melted and golden brown on top.

Squeeze lemon on top and serve immediately with Greek bread.

½ lb. kasseri cheese

juice of ½ lemon

2 tsps. olive oil

Per Serving: Calories: 222, Protein: 11 gm., Fat:15 gm., Carbohydrates: 2 gm.

Fried Cheese Sticks
Saghanaki
Serves 2

Saghanaki is a very popular appetizer in Greece. It gets its name from the two-handled shallow pan in which the cheese is fried and served.

Cut cheese into 2 strips, ½ inch thick and 3" long. In a frying pan melt butter and fry cheese on all sides until crusty and chestnut-colored. The cheese will melt a little. Sprinkle with lemon juice and serve immediately.

You can roll the strips in flour before you fry them if you wish.

¼ lb. kasseri cheese

2 Tbsps. butter

lemon juice

Per Serving: Calories: 273, Protein: 11 gm., Fat: 20 gm., Carbohydrates: 3 gm.

Eggplant Dip
Melitzanosalta

Makes 2 cups

This may be served as a salad as well as a dip.

1 large eggplant

1 onion, thinly sliced

2 cloves garlic, minced

1 Tbsp. parsley, chopped

¼ cup olive oil

2 Tbsps. red wine vinegar

½ tsp. salt

white pepper to taste

Puncture eggplant with a knife to prevent it from exploding while it bakes.

Place it in a baking dish or on aluminum foil and bake for about 1 hour in a preheated 350° oven. Dip eggplant into cold water to cool. Peel, cut in half and remove seeds, using a stainless steel knife to avoid discoloration.

Drain any excess liquid from eggplant halves.

Dice and transfer to a wooden bowl. Add onion, garlic, parsley, olive oil, vinegar, salt and pepper, and mix well. Chill for several hours so flavors may blend. As a dip, serve with crackers, radishes or carrot sticks. For a salad, spoon mixture onto leaves of romaine or iceberg lettuce and garnish with parsley and Greek olives.

Per 2 Tablespoon Serving: Calories: 35, Protein: 0, Fat: 3 gm., Carbohydrates: 1 gm.

Eggplant Tahini Dip
Melitzanosalta me Tahini

Makes 2 cups

Prepare eggplant as directed in *Eggplant Dip*, omitting the onion, garlic, parsley, olive oil and vinegar, and adding 3 Tbsps. tahini, and 3 Tbsps. lemon juice. Like Eggplant Dip, this may be served as a salad.

Per 2 Tbsps.Serving: Calories: 14, Protein: 1 gm., Fat 1 gm.,
Carbohydrates 1 gm.:

1 large eggplant

3 Tbsps. tahini

3 Tbsps. lemon juice

½ tsp. salt

white pepper to taste

French Fried Eggplant
Melitzanes Tiganites

Makes 4 servings

Wash eggplant, pare and cut into strips the size of a finger. Season with salt and pepper. Roll in bread crumbs and fry in deep hot oil until golden and crispy.

Per Serving: Calories: 165, Protein: 2 gm., Fat: 12 gm.,
Carbohydrates: 10 gm.

1 large eggplant

1 cup bread crumbs

salt and pepper to taste

Stuffed Grape Leaves

Dolmathes Yalantzi

Makes 20 to 25

Dolmathes are the appetizer most favored by hostesses and chefs throughout Greece. The leaves of the grapevines are very tender in the spring. Stuffed with onions, rice and spices, dolmathes are just the right shape and size to serve to your guests before dinner. If you can not find fresh leaves you can use those in jars, as I mention in the recipe.

1 (16 oz.) jar grape leaves

1 Tbsp. olive oil

3 medium onions, chopped

½ cup parsley, chopped

2 Tbsps. fresh dill, chopped, or 1 Tbsp. dried dill

¾ cup uncooked rice

1 Tbsp. dried mint

salt to taste (about ½ tsp.)

pepper to taste

juice of 1½ lemon

¼ cup pine nuts (optional)

Rinse grape leaves thoroughly to remove brine and set aside.

Heat oil and sauté the chopped onions until soft. Stir in parsley, dill, rice, mint, salt, pepper, the juice of one lemon and pine nuts, if desired. Stir while cooking for 2-3 minutes over low heat. Remove from heat and let cool.

Pick out 7-8 of the thickest grape leaves and line the bottom of a 4 quart saucepan with them. They will protect the stuffed grape leaves from burning. You can also use a few sliced carrots if you prefer. Cut off thick stems from the remaining grape leaves. Place 1 teaspoon filling on underside of each leaf near stem end and fold base of leaf over filling. Then fold sides to enclose filling. Roll lightly toward point of leaf, so there will be room for the rice to cook and expand. Layer stuffed grape leaves seam-sides down on the grape leaves covering the bottom of the saucepan.

Add remaining lemon juice. If you have left-over grape leaves, these can be placed over the top of the stuffed leaves. Place an inverted plate on top of every-thing, then add enough water to cover (about 1 to 1½). Bring to a boil, then cover the pan, lower the heat and simmer as slowly as possible for 1¼ hours. Taste one to see if the rice is tender, and, if necessary, continue cooking slowly. Cool to room temperature and serve.

Hint: A 16 oz. jar of grape leaves should contain enough leaves so you could easily double the filling ingredients and make twice as many rolls.

Per Dolma: Calories: 28, Protein: 1 gm., Fat: 1 gm., Carbo hydrates: 5 gm.

Herbed Feta Cheese

Aromatiki Feta

Makes 1½ cups

Use as a spread on crackers.

Slice feta in large chunks and soak in cold water for 24 hours. Change the water every 4-5 hours. Drain, pat dry and place it in a large jar.

Add all ingredients, cover and shake to evenly distribute the herbs and oil.

This can be stored in refrigerator for a week.

Per Tablespoon Serving: Calories: 90, Protein: 4 gm., Fat: 8 gm., Carbohydrates: 1 gm.

1 lb. feta cheese

1 Tbsp. coriander

1½ Tbsps. rosemary

1 tsp. thyme

1 large clove garlic, split in two

3 black peppercorns

2 Tbsps. olive oil

Cheese Pie
Tyropitta
Serves 12

3 Tbsps. butter

3 Tbsps. flour

2 cups hot milk

1 lb. feta cheese,
   crumbled,
   or ½ lb. ricotta and
   ½ lb. tofu, crum-
   bled, plus 1 Tbsp.
   miso

1 tsp. dried mint

1 lb. phyllo pastry

½ cup butter,
   melted

In a saucepan melt 3 Tbsps. butter over low heat. Using a wire whisk stir in flour and blend well. Remove from heat. Gradually stir in milk to blend, then stir vigorously. Return to heat and cook until thickened. Let cool. Add feta cheese and mint and stir together to mix thoroughly.

Take half the phyllo sheets (about 14) from the package. Center 4 sheets in a buttered 9" x 13" baking pan and brush lightly with melted butter. Layer the rest of the sheets one by one on top of each other, brushing each layer. The sheets will extend up the sides of the pan. Spoon in the filling and spread evenly. Fold overhanging sides and ends of phyllo over the filling to enclose it. Brush lightly with melted butter. Top with phyllo sheets remaining in the package. Brush with melted butter as you layer them in the pan. Tuck overhanging edges around the inside of the baking pan to seal in filling. Using the point of a sharp knife score the surface lengthwise into 3 strips and bake in a preheated 325° oven until crisp and golden, about 1 hour.

If it seems to be browning too quickly reduce the temperature to 275°.

Remove from oven and let stand for 10 minutes. Cut through scored lines and cut again crosswise to make 12 rectangular pieces. Serve warm.

Per Serving: Calories: 333, Protein: 11 gm., Fat: 17 gm., Carbohydrates: 29 gm.

Spinach Triangles
Trighona me Spanaki
Makes 30 to 35 triangles

Squeeze spinach as dry as possible and place in a colander so that remaining moisture will drip out. It is important that spinach be dry.

Heat 1 Tbsp. olive oil and sauté the onions and scallions until soft. Add well-squeezed spinach, dill and parsley, and cook for 5 minutes, stirring constantly. Remove from heat and stir in feta cheese. Let cool.

Cut, fill and fold phyllo pastry as directed in *Baked Cheese Puffs* (see page 15), except brush strips with oil instead of butter.

Place the triangles in a baking pan and brush with oil. Bake in a preheated 350° oven until golden, about 20 minutes. Serve hot, or let cool, chill and serve cold.

Hint: This is an easy recipe to double and prepare for a large party. If you choose to freeze unbaked Spinach Triangles and heat later, remember to brush them with oil, not butter, before baking them.

Per Triangle: Calories: 61, Protein: 2 gm., Fat: 3 gm., Carbohydrates: 6 gm.

2 (10 oz.) pkgs. frozen chopped spinach (thawed)

1 Tbsp. olive oil

2 onions, chopped

1 bunch scallions, finely chopped (including 4" green tops)

¼ cup fresh dill, chopped, or 1½ Tbsps. dried dill

¼ cup fresh parsley, chopped

½ lb. feta cheese, crumbled, or ¼ lb. feta and ¼ lb. tofu, crumbled, plus 1 Tbsp. miso

½ lb. phyllo pastry

¼ cup olive or vegetable oil

Stuffed Cucumbers

Angouria Gemista

Serves 6 (about 36 slices)

3 cucumbers, 8"-10" long

¼ lb. feta cheese, crumbled

¼ cup cream cheese

2 Tbsps. parsley, finely chopped

2 Tbsps. dill, chopped

10 black olives, pitted and chopped

2 Tbsps. low or non-fat mayonnaise

pepper to taste

After peeling the cucumbers, cut them in half lengthwise. Scoop out the seeds and some of the cucumber. Mix all the other ingredients very well and fill the cucumbers with the mixture. Put the two parts of the cucumber back together so it looks whole and chill.

Cut into slices about ⅔ inches thick and serve as an appetizer.

Per Serving: Calories: 158, Protein: 9 gm., Fat: 4 gm., Carbohydrates: 4 gm.

Tomatoes a la Russe
Ntomates a la Russe

Serves 6

Select firm round tomatoes. Cut out the stem end and scoop out a little pulp. Sprinkle insides of tomatoes with salt. Place in refrigerator stem-ends-down to chill. When cold, slice into 6 sections but do not cut all the way through. Stuff each tomato with about a tablespoon of Russian Salad. Arrange on a platter and garnish with parsley.

6 medium tomatoes

salt

1 cup Russian Salad, page 53

sprigs of parsley

Per Serving: Calories: 67, Protein: 3 gm., Fat: 2 gm., Carbohydrates: 10 gm.

Soups

Bean Soup
Fasolatha

Serves 6

Fasolatha is a Greek national dish. It can be found in homes both in cities and villages from late fall through the winter. The Greeks can make a feast with this soup, serving it with olives, feta cheese, Greek bread, a good wine and fruit.

Wash beans and soak overnight in water to cover. The next morning rinse and drain. Transfer to a large 4 quart pot and add 9 cups water. Bring to a boil, lower heat, cover and cook for 1 hour.

Add the remaining ingredients and cook, covered, for 1 to 1½ hours. If soup is too thick add cold water and boil for a few minutes longer.

Per Serving: Calories: 116, Protein: 5 gm., Fat: 0 gm., Carbohydrates: 24 gm.

½ lb. (1 cup) dried white beans

9 cups cold water

2 large onions, sliced

2 cloves garlic, sliced

5 carrots, sliced

2 stalks celery, sliced

1 (8 oz.) can tomato sauce

2 Tbsps. parsley, chopped

1 tsp. salt

½ tsp. pepper

Chick Pea Soup
Revithia Soupa
Makes 6 servings

Chick pea soup is a Greek basic. We put in onions to thicken the soup, adding olive oil in the beginning of cooking and salt at the end to add to the flavor.

1 cup dried chick peas

6 cups cold water

2 onions, thinly sliced

1 Tbsp. olive oil

1 tsp. salt

lemon juice or wine vinegar

Wash and soak chick peas overnight in water to cover. The next day rinse and drain. In a 4 quart saucepan bring 6 cups of water to a boil and add the chick peas.

Remove the froth, then add the onion and olive oil. Simmer until tender, about 1-2 hours. Add salt at the end and hot water (not cold), if needed to make more stock.

Serve hot with lemon juice or vinegar.

Per Serving: Calories: 80, Protein: 3 gm., Fat: 2 gm., Carbohydrates: 12 gm.

Lentil Soup
Soupa Phakes
Serves 4 to 6

Lentils are a good source of iron. This healthy soup is popular throughout Greece in the winter months.

Pick over lentils, discarding any that are shrivelled or any stones, and rinse in a colander. Drain and transfer to a 4 quart saucepan. Add 8 cups water.

Stud onion with cloves; add onion, garlic, celery, tomatoes, parsley and bay leaf to lentils. Bring to a boil, lower heat, cover and cook for 30-50 minutes.

Add salt and pepper and cook for 10 minutes more, or until lentils are soft. If soup is too thick, add more cold water and cook for 5 minutes longer. Remove the bay leaf.

Serve with the vinegar so that each person may add it to his own taste. Leftover soup can be frozen.

Per Serving: Calories: 132, Protein: 7 gm., Fat: 0 gm., Carbohydrates: 27 gm.

½ lb. (1 cup) dried lentils

8 cups water

1 onion

6 whole cloves

3 cloves garlic

2 celery stalks, chopped

6 canned tomatoes, chopped, with the juice

4 sprigs fresh parsley, chopped

1 small bay leaf

salt and pepper to taste

wine vinegar

Lentil Soup with Spinach
Soupa Phaki me Spanaki

Serves 4 to 6

½ lb. (1 cup) dried
   lentils

4 cups water

1 lb. fresh spinach,
   or 1 (10 oz.) pack-
   age frozen
   spinach, thawed

2 Tbsps. olive oil

1 bunch scallions,
   chopped (includ-
   ing about 4" green
   tops)

2 cloves garlic, thin-
   ly sliced

salt and pepper to
   taste

Pick over lentils, discarding any that are shriv-elled or any stones, and rinse in a colander. Drain and transfer to a 4 quart saucepan. Add 4 cups water and bring to a boil. Lower heat, cover and cook until soft, about 30-50 minutes.

As the lentils cook wash the spinach thoroughly. Remove and discard coarse stems, cut the leaves in half and place in a colander to drain. If using frozen spinach, thaw and drain.

Heat olive oil and sauté the scallions until soft. Add them with the oil to the cooked lentils. Add garlic and spinach and cook for 15 minutes. Season with salt and pepper.

*Per Serving: Calories: 117, Protein: 6 gm., Fat: 5 gm.,
   Carbohydrates: 13 gm.*

Onion Soup
Kremydosoupa

Makes 4 servings

Fry onions in oil until golden brown. Add hot water, salt and pepper, and simmer for 10 minutes. Mix cornstarch with a little water and pour into soup. Stir for a few minutes until it thickens a little. Toast slices of bread and put one on each soup plate. Pour soup on top and sprinkle generously with the grated cheese.

Variations: Small croutons fried in butter or oil may also be used instead of toasted bread. Or before serving, the soup can be placed into oven proof bowls in a hot oven with toast and a slice of cheese on top until cheese is softened.

Per Serving: Calories: 250, Protein: 13 gm., Fat: 12 gm., Carbo-hydrates: 17 gm.

1 cup onions, chopped

2 Tbsps. olive oil

6 cups hot water

salt and pepper to taste

1 tsp. cornstarch

4 slices bread

½ cup parmesan cheese, grated

Split Pea Soup
Fava

Makes 4 servings

1 cup split peas

2 large onions,
   chopped

1 Tbsp. olive oil

2 cloves garlic,
   chopped

½ tsp. salt

Wash the split peas and place in a 4 quart soup pot with warm water to cover. Add the onions, olive oil, garlic and salt. Bring to a boil, cover and simmer for 45-50 minutes or until very soft. It is very important to stir the soup occasionally to keep it from burning. Serve warm or cold with lemon juice.

*Per Serving: Calories: 120, Protein: 5 gm., Fat: 3 gm.,
   Carbohydrates: 18 gm.*

Tahini Soup

Tahinosoupa

Serves 4

Rice can be used to make this soup if orzo is not available.

Bring water and 1 teaspoon salt to a boil in a 4 quart saucepan. Stir in tomato paste. Add orzo and boil for 25 minutes. While orzo boils, combine tahini and ½ cup cold water and beat with a fork. Gradually add lemon juice.

Before the soup is done take 1 cup of the hot broth and stir it slowly into the tahini mixture. When the soup is ready, stir the tahini mixture into it and season with salt and pepper. Serve hot.

Per Serving: Calories: 84, Protein: 3 gm., Fat: 6 gm., Carbohydrates: 9 gm.

6 cups water

1 tsp. salt

1 Tbsp. tomato paste

½ cup orzo (see page 7)

½ cup tahini

½ cup cold water

juice of one lemon

salt and pepper to taste

Tomato-Rice Soup

Ntomatosoupa

Makes 4 servings

2 Tbsps. butter
or olive oil

2 large onions,
chopped

1 green pepper,
chopped

6 medium tomatoes,
peeled, seeded and
chopped

½ cup uncooked rice

4 cups water

½ tsp. salt

¼ tsp. pepper

4 Tbsps. fresh
parsley, chopped

Sauté the onions and green pepper in butter or oil for about 3-5 minutes. Add the tomatoes and rice and cook for 5 more minutes. Add water, salt, pepper, and parsley. Bring to a boil. Reduce the heat and simmer for 30 minutes. If you wish, serve with sour cream on top.

Per Serving: Calories: 169, Protein: 5 gm., Fat: 6 gm.,
Carbohydrates: 25 gm.

Trahana Soup
Trahanosoupa
Serves 4

Trahana soup is a zesty peasant dish. You can find trahana in Greek and Syrian grocery stores or make it yourself from the recipe on page 135.

Sauté onions in butter or corn oil until soft. Add tomato sauce, garlic, parsley, bay leaf, salt and pepper. Cook until moisture is absorbed. Add trahana, stir and simmer until trahana is tender and has doubled in volume. Remove the bay leaf before serving and top with parmesan cheese.

Per Serving: Calories: 232, Protein: 6 gm., Fat: 6 gm., Carbohydrates: 29 gm.

2 onions, chopped

2 Tbsps. butter or corn oil

1 (8 oz.) can tomato sauce

2 cloves garlic, minced

¼ cup fresh parsley, chopped

1 bay leaf

½ tsp. salt

½ tsp. pepper

½ lb. trahana (see page 135)

6 cups hot water

½ cup parmesan cheese, grated

Summer Vegetable Soup
Kalo Kerini Hortosoupa

Serves 6

2 large onions,
chopped

1 bunch celery,
chopped

5 carrots, chopped

4 small zucchini,
chopped

3 leeks, chopped

½ cup lima beans,
fresh or frozen,
or ¼ cup soaked
dried lima beans

3 ripe tomatoes,
peeled and
chopped

2 Tbsps. fresh pars-
ley, chopped

½ tsp. salt

¼ tsp. pepper

croutons

Place all ingredients except croutons in an 8 quart pot. Cover with water and bring to a boil. Lower heat, cover and cook for 45 minutes. Serve topped with croutons.

*Per Serving: Calories: 119, Protein: 5 gm., Fat: 0 gm.,
Carbohydrates: 26 gm.*

Winter Vegetable Soup with Noodles

Himerini Hortosoupa

Makes 6 to 8 servings

Wash beans and soak overnight in enough water to cover. The next day rinse, drain and transfer to an 8 quart pot. Add 9 cups of water, bring to boil and simmer for 1 hour. Add carrots, celery, cabbage, onion, garlic, tomatoes, parsley, salt and pepper. Cook slowly for 10 minutes. Add potatoes and macaroni and cook ½ hour more. When all is done, let stand for 5-10 minutes, then serve.

Per Serving: Calories: 122, Protein: 5 gm., Fat: 0 gm., Carbohydrates: 26 gm.

½ cup dried white beans

½ cup dried red kidney beans

9 cups water

5 carrots, sliced

3-4 stalks of celery, diced

½ small cabbage, shredded

1 onion, sliced

2 cloves garlic, minced

1 (16 oz.) can tomatoes

2 Tbsps. fresh parsley, chopped

salt and pepper to taste

1 potato, diced

½ cup uncooked elbow macaroni

Yogurt Soup
Yaourtosoupa
Serves 6

¼ cup walnuts

2 cloves garlic

2 Tbsps. olive oil

2 Tbsps. white wine
vinegar

3 cups lowfat yogurt

1 cup skim milk

1 cucumber, peeled
and cut into small
cubes

salt and pepper to
taste

3 Tbsps. fresh
parsley, chopped

In a blender combine walnuts, garlic, olive oil and vinegar. Blend until smooth. Pour into a mixing bowl and stir in yogurt and milk. Keep stirring until smooth. Add cucumber and season with salt and pepper. Refrigerate. Just before serving, sprinkle with parsley.

Per Serving: Calories: 162, Protein: 8 gm., Fat: 9.5 gm., Carbohydrates: 11 gm.

Salads

White Bean Salad
Fasolia Salata
Serves 4

Take the garlic and mash well with a little salt. Add vinegar, oil, salt and pepper and mix well. Pour this mixture on warm beans, stir gently and chill.
Serve cold with chopped parsley or dill.

Per Serving: Calories: 176, Protein: 7 gm., Fat: 7 gm., Carbohydrates: 21 gm.

2 cups warm cooked white beans

1 clove garlic

2 Tbsps. wine vinegar

2 Tbsps. olive oil

salt and pepper to taste

2 Tbsps. fresh parsley or dill, chopped

Beet Salad
Patzaria Salata
Serves 2

1 bunch beets (4 or 5 medium beets)

1 Tbsp. salt

3 Tbsps. wine vinegar

1 Tbsp. olive oil

1 Tbsp. water

Remove the leaves and stalks from the beets. Scrub well under cold running water to remove all sand.

Place beets in a saucepan, cover with cold water, add salt and 1 Tbsp. vinegar. Bring to a boil, cover and cook until tender, about 45 minutes, or pressure cook about 5 to 7 minutes. Drain. Slip the beet skins off with your fingers and slice beets into a bowl. Toss with olive oil, water and 2 Tbsps. vinegar and serve warm; or let cool, chill and serve cold.

Beet salad goes very well with *Garlic Sauce*, page 61.

Note: For a different beet salad, boil the thoroughly washed leaves of the beets at the same time and toss them with the sliced beets.

Per Serving: Calories: 117, Protein: 2 gm., Fat: 7 gm., Carbohydrates: 13 gm.

Black-Eyed Pea Salad
Mavromatika Fasolia Salata

Serves 4 to 6

Cook frozen peas according to package directions and drain, or open and drain cooked canned peas. Combine with the onion, olive oil and vinegar.

Sprinkle with chopped parsley. Let cool and chill. Serve cold.

Note: *If you want to use dried peas, cook 2 cups covered with water in an uncovered saucepan for 45-60 minutes, or pressure cook at 15 lbs. pressure for 8 minutes.*

Per Serving: Calories: 153, Protein: 6 gm., Fat: 5 gm.,
    Carbohydrates: 20 gm.

3 (10 oz.) packages frozen black-eyed peas, or 2 (15 oz.) cans cooked black-eyed peas

1 large red or white onion, very thinly sliced

2 Tbsps. olive oil

2 Tbsps. wine vinegar

2 Tbsps. fresh parsley, chopped

Cabbage Salad
Lachanosalata
Serves 5 to 6

Crisp cabbage is a welcome change in the winter from the usual cooked vegetables. This salad is attractive and tasty. The Greek word for cabbage is lachano, *which developed into the word for vegetables,* lachanika.

1 small cabbage (about 1½ lbs.)

1 carrot, shredded

2 Tbsps. wine vinegar

salt and pepper to taste

¼ to ½ cup yogurt

¼ to ½ cup low or non-fat mayonnaise

Discard the outer leaves of the cabbage. Cut in half, remove the core and shred remaining leaves. Place in a large bowl and add carrots. Sprinkle with vinegar and season with salt and pepper. Combine the yogurt with the mayonnaise and add to the cabbage, mixing well. Chill and serve cold.

Per Serving: Calories: 93, Protein: 1 gm., Fat: 6 gm., Carbohydrates: 7 gm.

Cucumber-Yogurt Salad
Tzatziki
Serves 4

Use as a side dish or as a dip with pita bread.

Combine olive oil, vinegar, garlic, salt and pepper, and mix well. In a bowl, blend together yogurt and sour cream. Combine this mixture with the oil mixture. Add cucumbers and mix thoroughly. Chill. Just before serving, sprinkle with dill. Garnish with thin slices of cucumber, if desired.

Per Serving: Calories: 117, Protein: 2 gm., Fat: 8 gm., Carbohydrates: 5 gm.

1 Tbsp. olive oil

1 Tbsp. wine vinegar

2 cloves garlic, chopped

½ tsp. salt

¼ tsp. white pepper

½ cup yogurt

½ cup sour cream

2 cucumbers, peeled, seeded and diced

1 tsp. fresh dill, chopped, or ¼ tsp. dried dill

thinly sliced, peeled cucumber (optional)

Greek Salad
Salata Horiatiki
Serves 4 to 6

1 head romaine let-
tuce, cut into bite-
sized pieces

3 tomatoes, chopped

1 onion, sliced

1 green pepper,
seeded and sliced

1 cucumber, peeled
and sliced

1 cup black olives

¼ lb. feta cheese, cut
into chunks

Greek Salad
Dressing (see
below)

Chill all vegetables, the olives and cheese. Combine dressing ingredients. When ready to serve, toss all vegetables and the olives, and top with feta. You can pour the dressing on top or let your guests use as much as they want.

Per Serving (without dressing): Calories 143, Protein: 5 gm., Fat: 10 gm., Carbohydrates: 10 gm.

Greek Salad Dressing
Makes one third cup

2 Tbsps. olive oil
2 Tbsps. water
2 Tbsps. wine
vinegar
generous pinch of
oregano
salt and pepper to
taste

Combine ingredients, shake well and serve.

Per Tbsp. Serving: Calories: 48, Protein: 0 gm., Fat: 5 gm., Carbohydrates: 0 gm.

Green Pepper Salad

Pipperies Salata

Serves 4

Combine olive oil and the lemon juice. Blend well, add garlic and set aside.

Place peppers in a baking pan and bake in a preheated 400° oven until the skins are shriveled and blistered about 40 minutes. Let cool until you can handle them.

Slip off the skins, slice peppers into strips and remove seeds. Transfer strips to a bowl. Season with salt and pepper, pour on the olive oil mixture and stir. Sprinkle with parsley. Serve warm or cold.

Per Serving: Calories: 86, Protein: 1 gm., Fat: 7 gm., Carbohydrates: 6 gm.

2 Tbsps. olive oil

juice of one lemon

1 clove garlic, cut in half

5 green peppers

salt and pepper to taste

2 Tbsps. fresh parsley, finely chopped

Lentil Salad
Phakes Salata

Serves 6

1 cup dried lentils

6 cups water

1 onion, peeled

1 whole clove

2 cloves garlic

1 small bay leaf

salt to taste

2 Tbsps. olive oil

1 Tbsp. wine vinegar

1 onion, sliced and
separated into
rings

¼ cup fresh parsley,
chopped

Pick over lentils, discarding any that are shriveled or any stones, and rinse in a colander. Drain and transfer to a large saucepan. Add water. Stick peeled onion with clove and add them with the garlic and bay leaf to the pan. Bring to a boil, lower heat, cover and cook for 30-40 minutes. Ten minutes before the lentils are tender, add salt.

Drain, remove bay leaf and onion. Place lentils in a bowl and pour the oil and vinegar over them. Place onion rings on lentils and sprinkle with chopped parsley. Serve warm or cool.

*Per Serving: Calories: 97, Protein: 3 gm., Fat: 5 gm.,
Carbohydrates: 12 gm.*

Pickled Onions
Kremmithakia Marinata
Serves 4

Peel onions, and with a sharp knife cut two criss-cross slashes on the root end of each. This will keep them whole while cooking. In a saucepan combine the water, wine, oil, lemon juice, salt, peppercorns and bay leaf. Bring to a boil, then reduce heat and simmer for 3 minutes. Add the onions and cook over low heat for 25-30 minutes.

Serve cold.

If fresh pearl onions are not available, 1 (15 oz.) can onions can be used. Drain and rinse them and reduce the cooking time.

Per Serving: Calories: 107, Protein: 2 gm., Fat: 7 gm., Carbohydrates: 15 gm.

1 lb. small pearl onions*

¾ cup water

½ cup white wine

2 Tbsps. olive oil

juice of two lemons

½ tsp. salt

12 peppercorms

1 bay leaf

Potato Salad
Patatosalata

Makes 4 servings

4 medium potatoes

1 bunch scallions, finely sliced

1 tsp. oregano

salt and pepper to taste

2 Tbsps. olive oil

3 Tbsps. wine vinegar

Scrub the potatoes very well and steam for 30 minutes. Cool and dice them with the skin on. Add scallions, oregano, salt, pepper, oil, vinegar and mix well.

Serve cold.

Per Serving: Calories: 191, Protein: 4 gm., Fat: 7 gm., Carbohydrates: 30 gm.

Radish Salad
Repanakia me Yaourti Salata

Serves 3 to 4

1 Tbsp. red wine vinegar

1 tsp. sugar

1 tsp. salt

pepper to taste

½ cup sour cream

½ cup yogurt

24 medium radishes, cut crosswise into slices ⅛ inch thick

1 small red onion, cut into rings ⅛ inch thick

Combine vinegar, sugar, salt and pepper in a bowl and stir thoroughly. Beat in sour cream and yogurt a few tablespoons at a time. Stir in radishes and onion. Chill.

Per Serving: Calories: 120, Protein: 3 gm., Fat: 5 gm., Carbohydrates: 9 gm.

Russian Salad, Greek Style
Rossiki Salata
Serves 8 to 10

Extra salad can be used to stuff tomatoes for Tomatoes a la Russe, *page 25.*

Chill all vegetables. Combine potatoes, beets, carrots, green beans, peas and white beans in a large bowl and season with salt and pepper. Add parsley, pickles, capers and dill. Sprinkle on vinegar and lemon juice. Toss ¾ cup mayonnaise with the salad. Spread the reserved ¼ cup mayonnaise over the salad. If desired, garnish with sliced tomatoes and olives.

Per Serving: Calories: 206, Protein: 4 gm., Fat: 11 gm., Carbohydrates: 20 gm.

2 cups boiled potatoes, cubed

1 cup cooked beets, cubed

1 cup cooked carrots, cubed

1 cup cooked green beans, chopped

1 cup cooked peas

1 cup cooked white beans

salt and pepper to taste

2 Tbsps. fresh parsley, chopped

1 Tbsp. pickles, chopped

1 Tbsp. capers

1 Tbsp. fresh dill, chopped, or 1 tsp. dried dill

2 Tbsps. wine vinegar

juice of ½ lemon

1 cup low or non-fat mayonnaise

tomatoes and Greek olives (optional)

Sesame Dressing
Tahini Salata

Makes 2½ cups

3 garlic cloves,
  finely chopped

1 tsp. salt

1 cup tahini

1 cup cold water

½ cup lemon juice

With the back of a large spoon, mash the garlic with the salt. Stir in the tahini. Beat in half of the water and all the lemon juice. Still beating, add the rest of the water, one teaspoon at a time, until dressing has the consistency of mayonnaise.

Use as an ingredient in *Humus*, see pg. 92, a dressing in salads or over fried vegetables.

Per Tbsp: Calories: 20, Protein: 1 gm., Fat: 2 gm., Carbohydrates: 1 gm.

Spinach Salad
Spanakosalata
Makes 4 servings

Wash the spinach thoroughly. Cut the stems and leaves into pieces. Place in a large bowl, add the tomato, onion and feta cheese. Combine the dressing ingredients, shake well and pour over the salad.

Toss well and serve.

Per Serving: Calories: 181, Protein: 9 gm., Fat: 12 gm., Carbohydrates: 10 gm.

1 lb. fresh spinach

1 tomato, sliced

½ medium onion, thinly sliced

¼ lb. feta cheese, crumbled, or ¼ lb. tofu plus 1 Tbsp. miso

DRESSING
2 Tbsps. olive oil
2 Tbsps. water
3 Tbsps. wine vinegar
½ tsp. oregano
salt and pepper to taste

String Bean Salad
Fasolakia Freska Salata

Serves 4

2 Tbsps. olive oil

2 Tbsps. water

3 Tbsps. lemon juice

1 clove garlic, cut in
half

1 lb. fresh string
beans

1 tsp. salt

4 cups water

1 Tbsp. fresh parsley,
chopped

In a small jar combine the oil and water with the lemon juice and garlic. Shake well and let stand.

Remove the ends and strings from the beans, but do not cut up the beans themselves. Add the salt to the water, bring to a boil and drop in the beans. Cook until tender, about 10-25 minutes. Drain. Place in a bowl, pour in the dressing and parsley, and mix gently. Serve warm or cold.

*Per Serving: Calories: 94, Protein: 2 gm., Fat: 7 gm.,
Carbohydrates: 8 gm.*

Tomato and Cucumber Salad
Ntomato-Angourosalata

Serves 4

3 or 4 ripe tomatoes

1 cucumber, peeled
and thinly sliced

½ onion, thinly
sliced

2 Tbsps. olive oil

½ tsp. oregano

salt and pepper to
taste

Greek bread

Cut the tomatoes into small pieces or thin slices. Combine with cucumber, onion, olive oil, oregano, salt and pepper. Mix well and chill. Serve with slices of Greek bread for dipping into the sauce.

*Per Serving: Calories: 105, Protein: 2 gm., Fat: 7 gm.,
Carbohydrates: 9 gm.*

Boiled Wild Greens Salad
Vrasta Agria Horta
Serves 2

A great variety of wild greens grow in abundance in the Greek fields. They are dug up, sometimes roots and all, by the women of the villages and taken home to be boiled that very day. Here in America some of the same greens can be found in supermarkets.

Remove the roots of each plant. Wash the greens very thoroughly under cold running water, separating the leaves to get rid of every bit of sand. Drain. Place the leaves in an 8 quart pot filled three-quarters with lightly salted water. Bring to a boil and simmer very rapidly, uncovered, until tender. The time varies with the variety of greens. Drain, let cool and chill. Serve with a sprinkle of olive oil and lemon juice.

Note: *Reserve the cooking water, add a bit of lemon juice and you will have a vitamin-filled drink my father told me about in Greece years ago—before vitamin pills.*

Per Serving: Calories: 62, Protein: 8 gm., Fat: 0 gm., Carbohydrates: 10 gm.

1 pound of any one of the following:

dandelion greens (radikia)

mustard greens (sinapia)

cress (kardamo)

beet greens (patjaro-phylla)

curly endive or escarole (antidia)

spinach (spanaki)

Swiss chard (seskoula)

kale

olive oil and lemon juice to taste

Zucchini Salad
Kolokithia Salata

Makes 3 servings

2 Tbsps. olive oil

2 Tbsps. lemon
juice

1 clove garlic, cut
in half

4-5 small zucchini

1 qt. water

¼ tsp. salt or to
taste

3-4 fresh dill
sprigs, chopped

In a small jar, combine the oil with the lemon juice and garlic. Shake well and let stand.

Wash the zucchini and trim off the ends. Cut into thick slices. Bring the water to a boil and add salt. Drop zucchini into water and cook uncovered over a moderate heat until tender. The zucchini can also be boiled or steamed whole, then cut.

Drain, place in a bowl and season with dill. Pour the dressing mix on gently.

Serve warn or cold.

*Per Serving: Calories: 107, Protein: 2 gm., Fat: 9 gm.,
Carbohydrates: 2 gm.*

Sauces

Garlic Sauce
Skorthalia
Makes 1¹/₂ cups

Skorthalia is a mainstay of Greek cookery. It goes wonderfully with fried eggplants, zucchini, beets and any kind of fried food. Traditionally it is made with a "goudi" (mortar and pestle), but you can make it in an electric blender or mixer.

Soak bread in water to cover, then squeeze as dry as possible. Crush garlic in mortar or garlic press and blend in salt. Transfer it to a blender, add bread and mix well. Add very small amounts of oil, vinegar and water alternately, blending constantly until each addition is well absorbed. Taste for seasoning, adding more vinegar or squeezed bread if necessary. Blend until sauce is thick and smooth, adding the juice of ½ lemon when done, if desired.

Place in a bowl, cover and chill until ready to serve. It will keep for a week in the refrigerator in sealed jars.

Note: Skordalia may also be made with a 16 oz. can of chick peas instead of bread slices.

12 slices dry white or wheat bread

5 cloves garlic

½ tsp. salt

¼ cup olive oil

⅓ cup wine vinegar

1 Tbsp. water

juice of ½ lemon (opt.)

Per Tablespoon serving: Calories: 51, Protein: 1 gm., Fat: 2 gm., Carbohydrates: 6 gm.

Garlic Sauce with Potatoes
Skorthalia Me Patates

Makes about 3 cups

4 medium potatoes

5 slices Italian bread,
cut 1" thick

6 cloves garlic

½ tsp. salt

¼ cup olive oil

⅓ cup lemon juice

1 Tbsp. water

Boil potatoes in a medium saucepan with just enough water to cover until soft, about 40 minutes. When cool enough to handle, slip skins or peel, and mash.

Soak bread in water to cover, then squeeze as dry as possible. Crush garlic in mortar or garlic press and blend in salt. Transfer to a blender, add hot mashed potatoes into garlic until well blended. Add bread and blend again. Add very small amounts of olive oil, lemon juice and water alternately, blending constantly after each addition is well absorbed, and the sauce is thick and smooth.

*Per ¼ Cup: Calories: 93, Protein: 2 gm., Fat: 5 gm.,
Carbohydrates: 11 gm.*

Lemon-Oil Dressing

Latholemono

Makes 1 cup

Latholemono is not only a good dressing for salads, but a topping for vegetables as well.

Combine all ingredients in a small jar and shake well. Let it stand at room temperature at least 1 hour before being used.

Per Tbsp: Calories: 60, Protein: 0 gm., Fat: 7 gm., Carbohydrates: 0 gm.

½ cup olive oil

juice of one large lemon

1 garlic clove, split

pinch of salt

pinch of pepper

¼ tsp. dried oregano

Homemade Mayonnaise
Mayonnaisa

Makes 1½ cups

This sauce was adopted from France where it was first made in the city of Mayen.

2 egg yolks from
large eggs,
or egg substitute

1 tsp. wine vinegar

½ tsp. salt

¼ tsp. white pepper

¼ tsp. mustard pow-
der (optional)

1 cup olive oil

¼ cup lemon juice

All ingredients and utensils should be at room temperature. Egg yolks or substitute should be out of the refrigerator for at least 1 hour. Beat egg yolks with a wire whisk until thick. Keep beating, always in one direction, and add vinegar, salt and pepper. Still beating, add olive oil, at first by drops (this is very important), then by teaspoons and finally by tablespoons, beating all the time. Wait until each addition is absorbed before adding the next. When the sauce thickens, gradually beat in the lemon juice.

An electric blender can be used with the same results. After beating the eggs, remove the top of the blender and slowly add the other ingredients, using the drop-by-drop technique.

*Per Tbsp: Calories: 87 Protein: 1 gm., Fat: 9 gm.,
Carbohydrates: 0 gm.*

Olive Oil and Vinegar Dressing
Lathoxytho

Makes 1 cup

Lathoxytho is a dressing of oil (lathi in Greek) and wine vinegar (xythi).
A Greek will always crumble a little oregano into the salad before tossing it.
Let it stand 1 hour at room temperature before using it.

Combine all ingredients in a small jar. Shake well and let stand at room temperature so the garlic can release its flavors. Store the leftover dressing in the refrigerator for future use.

Per Tbsp.: Calories: 61, Protein: 0 gm., Fat: 7 gm.,
Carbohydrates: 0 gm.

½ cup olive oil

½ cup wine vinegar

1 clove garlic, cut in half

pinch of oregano

pinch of salt

Parsley Dressing
Mantanosalata

Makes 1 1/4 cups

6 large bunches of parsley

2 Tbsps. corn flour

1 cup plus 2 Tbsps. water

2 Tbsps. olive oil

2 Tbsps. lemon juice

salt and pepper to taste

Rinse parsley well in cold water and drain. Pluck off leaves, discarding stems. Using scissors or a sharp knife cut up parsley leaves very fine.

In a saucepan, mix corn flour and water and bring to a boil, stirring constantly. Simmer for 2 minutes. Transfer to a blender and add parsley, oil, lemon juice, salt and pepper and blend until smooth.

Use as a dip with pita bread, carrots, radishes etc.

Per Tbsp: Calories: 10, Protein: 0 gm., Fat: 1 gm.,
Carbohydrates: 0 gm.

Tahini Sauce
Tahini Saltsa

Makes 3 cups

Beat well all ingredients with a whisk or in a blender. Chill. Serve with pita bread, crackers, radishes or carrot sticks.

Per Tbsp: Calories: 29, Protein: 1 gm., Fat: 2 gm., Carbohydrates: 1 gm.

1½ cups tahini

1½ cups yogurt

1 clove garlic, minced

½ cup lemon juice

3-4 scallions, chopped

¼ parsely, finely minced

Tomato Sauce
Saltsa Ntomata

Makes 4 cups

Mince 1 clove garlic. Heat olive oil and sauté minced garlic and the onions until soft. Add tomatoes, tomato paste, oregano, 4 cloves garlic split in half, the salt and pepper. Bring to a boil and simmer for 1 hour or until sauce thickens, stirring frequently. Serve hot on spaghetti or rice.

Per Cup: Calories: 192, Protein: 6 gm., Fat: 7 gm., Carbohydrates: 29 gm.

5 cloves garlic

2 Tbsps. olive oil

3 onions, chopped

1 (32 oz.) can tomatoes

1 (7 oz.) can tomato paste

2 tsps. oregano

1½ tsps. salt

½ tsp. pepper

Yogurt
Yaourti
Makes 4 cups

*Yogurt is a Turkish word for fermented milk. It can be eaten as a separate course,
with meals, in salads or in the cooking of other Greek dishes.
It goes particularly well with rice or* Pligouri *(see page 140).*

1 quart low-fat milk

**3 tablespoons plain
    yogurt to use as
    starter**

Bring the milk to a boil and simmer for 2-3 minutes, stirring constantly. Pour into an earthenware or
porcelain bowl and let cool. If a food thermometer is
available, it should read 130°. If a thermometer is not
available, test a drop of milk on your wrist; it should
be lukewarm. Cold milk will bring unsuccessful
results.

Mix a few tablespoons of the warm milk with the
yogurt and stir the mixture back into the milk. Cover
the bowl; wrap snugly in a towel or blanket and allow
to stand undisturbed in a warm, quiet place for 4 to 12
hours or overnight.

If you wish to have a really thick yogurt the way
the Greek mountain or island people do, cut a square
of clean muslin and make a bag about 6" x 12". Spoon
the yogurt into the bag and hang over a bowl placed
in the kitchen sink. The bowl will collect the whey, the
liquid that drips out, which is a very healthy drink.

Instead of making a bag, you can line a colander
with muslin or layers of cheesecloth. Place the colander in a bowl and spoon the yogurt into the cloth liner.
Every half-hour or so, pull up the 4 corners of the cloth
and squeeze the yogurt to encourage the whey to drip
out.

When the yogurt is ready, place in a bowl or glass

jar and chill. It can be kept in the refrigerator for more than a week. Be sure to save some yogurt to start the next batch.

You can also make yogurt in individual bowls, using a teaspoon of "starter" per bowl.

Per Cup: Calories: 95, Protein: 9 gm., Fat: 2 gm.,
Carbohydrates: 10 gm.

Entrees

Golden Breaded Artichoke Hearts
Anginares Pane
Serves 5

If you are using fresh whole artichokes, remove the leaves and chokes, leaving only the hearts. As you clean each one, rub the heart with the cut side of the lemon and then immerse heart in a bowl of cold water to which the juice of one lemon juice has been added. Let soak for 10 minutes. This process will prevent artichokes from darkening. It is not necessary with canned or frozen hearts.

Rinse and drain hearts, and then cut in half. Place in saucepan, add water to cover along with the remaining lemon juice and ½ tablespoon salt. Boil for 25 minutes drain, and cool. (15 minutes if using canned or frozen artichokes)

In a bowl, lightly beat eggs with ½ teaspoon salt and 2 tablespoons water. Place cheese in a deep plate and bread crumbs in a second deep plate. Dip the artichokes first in eggs, then in cheese, in eggs again and finally in bread crumbs. Heat butter and oil until sizzling and fry until golden on all sides.

Per Serving: Calories: 298, Protein: 14 gm., Fat: 14 gm.,
Carbohydrates: 26 gm.

10 fresh artichokes or 10 canned or frozen artichoke hearts (thawed)

2 lemons and their juice

½ Tbsp. salt

3 eggs or egg substitute

½ tsp. salt

2 Tbsps. water

¼ cup kefalotyri or parmesan cheese, grated

1 cup bread crumbs

2 Tbsps. butter

2 Tbsps. olive oil

Baked Beans
Fasolia Plaki
Makes 6 servings

1 cup dried navy beans

9 cups water

2 onions, chopped

2 cloves garlic, minced

2 Tbsps. olive oil

1 carrot, sliced thinly

1 stalk celery, chopped

3 Tbsps. fresh parsley, chopped

4 tomatoes, peeled and chopped, or 1 (16 oz.) can tomatoes

1 tsp. dry oregano

1 bay leaf

salt and pepper to taste

Wash beans and soak overnight in a 4 quart saucepan with enough water to cover. Next day, discard the water, rinse and drain. Add 9 cups of fresh water, bring to a boil and simmer for 1 hour.

Sauté the onions and garlic in the oil. Add carrots, celery, parsley and simmer for 10 minutes. Combine with tomatoes, beans, herbs, salt and pepper. Place them in a 4 quart ovenproof casserole, cover and bake in a slow oven (300°) for 1½-2 hours.

Per Serving: Calories: 168, Protein: 7 gm., Fat: 5 gm., Carbohydrates: 25 gm.

Beans in Tomato Sauce
Fasolia Yachni

Makes 6 servings

Wash beans and soak overnight in a 4 quart saucepan in enough water to cover. Next day, rinse and drain. Transfer to a large pot and add 8 cups of water. Bring to a boil, lower heat, cover and cook for one hour.

Sauté onions in olive oil. Add tomato sauce and pepper. Drain the beans, and while hot, add the tomato sauce. Cook until beans are soft, about ten minutes, and add salt and pepper. Serve warm.

Per Serving: Calories: 116, Protein: 4 gm., Fat: 5 gm., Carbohydrates: 16 gm.

1 cup dried navy beans

8 cups water

2 Tbsps. olive oil

2 onions, chopped

1 (8 oz.) can tomato sauce

salt and pepper to taste

Stuffed Cabbage Leaves
Lachanodolmathes

Serves 6

2 medium
cabbages

2 Tbsps. butter
or oil

3 onions,
chopped

1 cup chick peas

½ cup uncooked
rice

1 (16 oz.) can
tomato sauce

½ cup fresh
parsley,
chopped

2 cloves garlic,
minced

1 tsp. cinnamon

1 tsp. salt

½ tsp. pepper

1 cup boiling
water

juice of ½ lemon

lemon slices for
garnish

Discard torn or discolored outside leaves of cabbages. Remove the core, cutting as deeply as you can, and discard (or better still, eat it raw). Immerse cabbages, core-sides-down, into boiling salted water for 5 to 10 minutes, until just softened. If you wish, while they are boiling, add a crust of dried bread to the leaves to eliminate the strong odor of cabbage. Drain and set aside to cool while preparing the stuffing.

Heat 1 Tbsp. of the butter or oil and sauté the onions in a 4 quart saucepan. Add chick peas, rice, half the tomato sauce, the parsley, garlic, cinnamon, salt and pepper, and boiling water. Simmer until rice is half-done, approximately 10 minutes. Take off the cabbage leaves one by one. Line the bottom of an 8 quart pot with the first 4 to 5 thick leaves. They will prevent the stuffed leaves from burning.

Cut off the thick stems of the remaining leaves. Place 1 rounded tablespoon of chick pea mixture about ¼ inch above cut end of each leaf and fold cut end over filling. Then fold sides in to enclose filling; roll up lightly to give the rice room to expand as it continues to cook. Leftover cabbage leaves, if any, can be used for another dish.

Layer stuffed leaves, seam-sides-down, on the cabbage leaves covering the bottom of the pot. Dot with remaining butter or oil. Place an inverted heatproof plate directly on the stuffed leaves. Add remaining tomato sauce, the lemon juice and enough hot water to just cover the rim of the plate. Cover and simmer for 1½ hours. Serve warm with lemon slices.

Per Serving: Calories: 182, Protein: 7 gm., Fat: 4 gm., Carbohydrates: 31 gm.

Cheese Filled "Flutes"
Flogheres me Tyri
Makes 6 to 8 servings

Warm the butter. In a small bowl combine the cheese with the parsley. Mash them together with a fork until blended into a smooth paste.

Take a sheet of phyllo and fold in half crosswise. Brush with melted butter. Place 2 tablespoons of the cheese mixture at the narrow end and fold long sides in toward the middle to enclose the filling. Brush with butter and roll up into a tube shape or "flute." Brush with milk.

In a heavy 12" skillet heat 1-2 inches of oil until hot. Fry 4-5 flogheres at a time, turning them once with a slotted spoon until golden on both sides. Drain on paper towels and serve hot.

Hint: If you're expecting company, this is a great recipe to double. You can also make extra and store in the freezer. Enclose filling, butter and roll up. When ready to heat, brush with milk and fry according to recipe directions.

¼ cup clarified butter (see page 12)

½ lb. feta cheese or ¼ lb. ricotta and ¼ lb. tofu + 1 Tbsp. light miso

¼ cup fresh parsley, finely chopped

¼ lb. phyllo

¼ cup milk

1 cup vegetable oil for deep frying

Per Serving: Calories: 230, Protein: 7 gm., Fat: 18 gm., Carbohydrates: 12 gm.

Working with Eggplant

Your eggplant recipes will be less bitter if you soak the eggplant in salted water before using. For one large eggplant, layer pieces or slices in a bowl just big enough to hold them. Add a tablespoon of salt while layering and cover eggplant with water, weighting it down with a plate.

After about 15 minutes, drain and rinse.

Eggplant au Gratin
Melitzanes o Graten

Makes 6 servings

2 lbs. eggplant
(about two 8" egg-
plants)

⅓ cup butter
or olive oil

½ cup grated
parmesan cheese

¼ cup bread crumbs

WHITE SAUCE
2 Tbsps. butter
3 Tbsps. flour
2 cups milk

Cut the eggplants in thick slices lengthwise. Soak in salted water for 15 minutes. Rinse and squeeze slices dry. Fry them in butter or oil until soft, then place them neatly in a 9" x 13" baking pan. To make the white sauce melt the butter in a saucepan and whisk in flour. Slowly add milk and whisk until thick. Mix sauce with the grated cheese and pour on top of the eggplants. Sprinkle with bread crumbs and bake in a hot oven until golden brown.

Per Serving: Calories: 238, Protein: 5 gm., Fat: 16 gm., Carbohydrates: 13 gm.

Eggplant Patties
Melitzanokephtethes

Makes 4 to 5 servings

Wash the eggplants and slit lengthwise in 2-3 places. Drop in boiling salted water and cook until soft. Drain well. Remove the skin and mash the pulp. Combine with bread crumbs, baking powder, onion, cheese, parsley, eggs, salt and pepper. Shape into patties or croquttes. Roll in extra bread crumbs and fry until golden.

Per Serving: Calories: 459, Protein: 17 gm., Fat: 29 gm., Carbohydrates: 26 gm.

2 large eggplants

1½ cups bread crumbs

1 tsp. baking powder

1 small onion, finely chopped

½ cup kefalotyri or parmesan cheese, grated

2 Tbsps. fresh parsley, chopped

2 eggs or egg substitute

salt and pepper to taste

more bread crumbs for rolling

oil for frying

Eggplant Tomato Soufflé
Melitzanes me Saltsa Se Forma
Makes 6 servings

2 lbs. eggplant
(about two 8" egg-
plants)

¼ cup olive oil

1 clove garlic,
minced

4 eggs or egg
substitute

½ cup milk

salt and pepper to
taste

SAUCE
2 lbs. soft
tomatoes
3 Tbsps. olive oil
1 onion
1 clove garlic
basil or bay leaf
salt and pepper to
taste

Cut the eggplant in small chunks, remove as many seeds as you can and soak in salted water for 15 minutes according to the directions on page 78. Rinse and squeeze dry. Sauté in oil until soft. Mash the chunks with a fork or in a blender, adding the garlic, well-beaten eggs, milk, salt and pepper.

Fill a well greased 8" x 8" baking pan (or two smaller pans that together hold the same amount) about ¾ full with the mixture. Cover and place in a pan of water and bake in a 350° oven for 1 hour.

In the meantime, cut the tomatoes and onion in slices and cook in oil with salt, pepper and herbs. If you wish, pass the tomatoes through a sieve. Cook the sauce until thick. Take the soufflé out of the oven, unmold, and pour the sauce on top. Instead of using one large baking pan, you can use different individual molds if you wish.

Per Serving: Calories: 251, Protein: 7 gm., Fat: 18 gm.,
Carbohydrates: 11 gm.

Baked Eggplant with Cheese
Melitzanes me Tyri Tou Fournou
Makes 4 to 6 servings

Cut the eggplant in thick slices. Soak them in salted water for 15 minutes according to the directions on page 78, then rinse and pat dry. Fry in oil on both sides until brown and place them in a 9" x 13" baking pan. Cover with sauce and parmesan cheese and bake in a 350° oven for 25-30 minutes.

Per Serving: Calories: 235, Protein: 7 gm., Fat: 11 gm., Carbohydrates: 27 gm.

2 large eggplants

¼ cup olive oil

4 cups Tomato Sauce, page 67

½ cup parmesan cheese, grated

Baked Eggplant with Tomatoes and Chick Peas

Melitzanes me Ntomates kai Revithia

Makes 6 servings

¼ cup olive oil

2 medium eggplants, cut into 2" cubes

3 onions, cut in thick slices

2 cloves garlic, minced

salt and pepper to taste

2 cans chick peas, drained and rinsed under cold water

1 (16 oz.) can tomatoes, chopped and drained

1½ cups hot water

Soak eggplant cubes according to the directions on page 78. In large skillet, heat the oil to just before the smoking point. Fry the eggplant cubes, stirring frequently until they are browned on all sides. Remove from pan.

Add the onions and garlic and sauté for 5 minutes, being careful not to burn. Place eggplant in a 9" x 13" baking pan. Add onions, garlic, salt and pepper. Scatter the chick peas on top and cover with the tomatoes. Pour in the hot water.

Bake in a preheated 400° oven for 45 minutes. Serve at room temperature.

Per Serving: Calories: 235, Protein: 7 gm., Fat: 11 gm., Carbohydrates. 27 gm.

Imam Baildi
Imam Baildi
Serves 4 to 6

Cut off and discard leaves of each eggplant but leave on a part of the stem. Make 2 to 3 deep slits in each eggplant without cutting all the way through. If you use medium eggplants, make 1 deep slit through the skin side of each quarter. Soak in salted water for 15 minutes according to the directions on page 78; rinse and drain. Squeeze out excess moisture and pat dry. Tuck a slice of garlic into each eggplant slit and set aside.

Pour enough olive oil into a frying pan to cover the bottom. Heat until a drop of water landing in it sizzles and fry eggplants lightly on all sides. Add more olive oil if necessary. Transfer eggplants neatly in one layer to a 9" x 13" baking pan.

In another frying pan heat 2 Tbsps. olive oil and sauté the onions until soft. Add tomatoes, parsley, mint, salt and pepper. Cook for 20 to 25 minutes. Stuff the mixture into the slits in each eggplant. Pour the rest on top.

Add a little water, cover and bake in a preheated 350° oven for 45 minutes. Let cool and serve cold.

Per Serving: Calories: 316, Protein: 4 gm., Fat: 27 gm., Carbohydrates: 17 gm.

3 lbs. (10-12) narrow eggplant, 4-6" long, or 3 medium eggplants quartered

5-6 cloves garlic, sliced

1 cup olive oil for frying

2 Tbsps. olive oil

4 onions, thinly sliced

1 (32 oz.) can tomatoes, sliced

1 cup fresh parsley, chopped

2 tsps. salt

1 tsp. dried mint

½ tsp. pepper

Imam Baildi Top of the Stove
Imam Baildi Stin Katsarola
This recipe is made without frying the eggplants, making a lighter dish.

Prepare the eggplants as directed in Imam Baildi, but do not fry. Set them aside. Heat 2 Tbsps. olive oil in a large pan and sauté the onions until soft. Add eggplants and stir to coat with oil. Add remaining ingredients. Cover and simmer for 1 hour. Let cool, and serve cold.

Per Serving: Calories: 126, Protein: 4 gm., Fat: 5 gm., Carbohydrates: 17 gm.

Moussaka

Moussaka

Serves 12

Moussaka is the best known Greek dish in America. It traveled to Greece from the Middle East as did many other Greek dishes. It is usually made with eggplants and chopped meat, especially lamb, but here I substituted chick peas for the chopped meat.

Moussaka is an excellent choice for entertaining because it can be prepared the day before and then reheated slowly in a 200° oven. If you make it in advance, cut it into squares just before you reheat it.

1 cup dried or 2 (16 oz.) cans chick peas, cooked

3 medium eggplants

¼ cup olive oil

3 onions, thinly sliced

2 Tbsps. olive oil

2 large tomatoes, skinned, seeded and chopped

3 Tbsps. fresh parsley, chopped

1 tsp. salt

½ tsp. pepper

½ tsp. cinnamon

Soak the dried chick peas overnight. The next morning drain, add fresh water, bring to a boil and cook for 50 minutes. Drain and chop. Cut off stems of each eggplant and discard. Cut eggplants lengthwise into ¼ inch slices. Immerse in salted water for about 15 minutes according to the directions on page 78. Rinse and drain the slices; squeeze out excess moisture and pat dry. Heat olive oil and fry eggplant slices lightly, adding olive oil if necessary.* Set eggplant aside. In a frying pan sauté the onions until soft. Add chopped chick peas, tomatoes, parsley, salt, pepper and cinnamon. Stir. Add half of the grated cheese and stir well.

Prepare the white sauce by melting butter over low heat in a small saucepan. Using a wire whisk, stir in flour and blend well. Remove from heat. Gradually stir in milk; then stir vigorously. Return to heat and cook, stirring constantly, until sauce is thick and smooth. Add salt. Add half of the remaining cheese. Set aside.

In a 9" x 13" baking dish sprinkle half of the bread crumbs and place half of the eggplant slices neatly on top. Cover completely with the chick pea mixture, spreading evenly with a spatula. Sprinkle with a little grated cheese. Layer the remaining eggplant slices over the chick peas. Spoon the sauce over the top and sprinkle with remaining bread crumbs and cheese. Bake in a preheated 350° oven until golden, about 45 minutes. Cool for 15 minutes; then cut.

Note: Instead of frying the eggplants, you can bake them in the oven. Brush slices with olive oil on both sides, place in well-oiled baking pans, and bake in a preheated 400° oven for ½ hour or until tender, turning once. If you are a real eggplant lover, you may prefer to make Moussaka with 4 pounds of eggplants, using the same amounts of all the other ingredients. You might need more oil for frying them.

Per Serving: Calories: 350, Protein: 20 gm., Fat: 22 gm., Carbohydrates: 21 gm.

(continued on next page)

1 cup kefalotyri or parmesan cheese, grated

½ cup bread crumbs

WHITE SAUCE
6 Tbsps. butter
5 Tbsps. flour
4 cups milk, warmed
salt to taste

Light Moussaka
Moussaka me Melitzanes ke Revithia
Makes 8 to 10 servings

This is a lighter, less rich dish, without cheese or cream sauce.

1½ cups dry
or 2 (16 oz.) cans
chick peas

⅓ cup olive oil

2 eggplants, about 1
lb each, cut into 2"
cubes

2 Tbsps. olive oil

3 onions, sliced

salt and pepper to
taste

4 cups canned toma-
toes, chopped and
drained

1 cup water

If using dry chick peas soak overnight in enough water to cover. Next day rinse and add enough water to cover completely. Cover and simmer for 1½ to 2 hours or until tender. Drain and set aside. If you are using canned chick peas, drain and rinse under cold water, then drain again.

Soak the eggplant cubes according to the directions on page 78.

In a heavy skillet heat ⅓ cup olive oil to just before the smoking point. Cook the eggplant cubes, stirring frequently, until lightly browned on all sides. With a slotted spoon transfer them to a 9" x 13" baking pan and spread them out evenly.

Sauté the onions in a skillet in 2 Tbsps. olive oil until soft. Spread the onions on top of the eggplant. Sprinkle with salt and pepper. Scatter the chick peas on top and cover them with the tomatoes. Sprinkle with salt and pepper. Pour in the water and bake in a preheated 400° oven for 45 minutes.

*Per Serving: Calories: 246, Protein: 8 gm., Fat: 11 gm.,
Carbohydrates: 27 gm.*

Moussaka with Rice
Moussaka me Ryzi
Serves 4 to 6

Soak the chick peas overnight in enough water to cover. The next day drain, add 6 cups fresh water and simmer until tender, about 1-2 hours. Drain and pass the chick peas through a food mill or processor so they become the consistency of chopped meat. In a large frying pan sauté the onion in the butter until soft. Add tomatoes, parsley, salt and pepper. Add chick peas and stir. Set aside.

Cut eggplant into ½ inch thick slices and immerse in salted water for 15 minutes according to the directions on page 78. While the eggplant is soaking bring 2 cups water to a boil, add 1 tsp. salt and the rice, cover and cook for 10 minutes. Rinse and drain eggplant slices, squeeze out the excess moisture and pat dry. Heat olive oil and fry eggplant slices lightly. Drain rice and transfer to a 9" x 13" baking dish. Cover with chick pea mixture and place eggplant slices neatly on top. Sprinkle with bread crumbs, drizzle with melted butter and sprinkle with cheese. Bake in a preheated 350° oven for ½ hour.

Per Serving: Calories: 440, Protein: 13 gm., Fat: 17 gm., Carbohydrates: 52 gm.

1 cup dried chick peas

1 onion, chopped

1 Tbsp. butter

4 tomatoes, peeled, seeded and sliced

2 Tbsps. parsley, chopped

1 tsp. salt

¼ tsp. pepper

2 large eggplants

2 cups water

1 tsp. salt

1 cup uncooked rice

¼ cup olive oil

½ cup bread crumbs

2 Tbsps. butter, melted

½ cup kefalotyri or parmesan cheese, grated

Stuffed Eggplant "Little Shoes"
Melitzanes "Papoutsakia"

Serves 6 to 8

As with the Stuffed Zucchini recipe that follows later, this is a dish that is popular throughout Greece. The dish is made with small eggplants so the product looks like "little shoes."

3 lbs. (10-12) narrow eggplants, 4-6" long

1 cup olive oil for frying

2 Tbsps. butter or olive oil

2 cups cooked chick peas

3 onions, thinly sliced

1 lb. ripe tomatoes, peeled, seeded and cut up

¼ cup fresh parsley, chopped

1 tsp. salt

¼ tsp. pepper

¼ cup bread crumbs

¼ cup kefalotyri cheese, grated

Cut off and discard leaves and stems of each eggplant. Cut eggplants in half lengthwise. Soak in salted water for 15 minutes according to the directions on page 78; rinse and drain. Squeeze out excess moisture and pat dry. Scoop a small amount of pulp out of each eggplant half in order to make a hollow for the filling.

Pour 1 cup olive oil into a frying pan to cover the bottom; heat until a drop of water landing in it sizzles, and fry eggplants lightly on both sides. Place eggplant halves neatly side by side in a 9" x 13" baking pan. Heat 2 Tbsps. butter or oil and sauté onions until soft. Add chick peas, tomatoes, parsley, slt and pepper, and simmer over low heat until all the liquid has been absorbed. Stuff each eggplant half with chick pea mixture.

To make the white sauce, melt butter in a saucepan over low heat. Using a wire whisk stir in flour and blend well. Remove from heat. Gradually stir in milk; then stir vigorously. Return to heat and cook, stirring constantly, until sauce is thick and smooth. Add salt and pepper if desired. Pour over stuffed eggplant halves. Sprinkle them with bread crumbs and grated cheese. Bake in a preheated 350° oven until golden brown, about 30-40 minutes.

WHITE SAUCE
2 Tbsps. butter
2 Tbsps. flour
1 cup milk, warmed
salt and pepper to taste

Per Serving: Calories: 319, Protein: 10 gm., Fat: 14 gm., Carbohydrates: 32 gm.

Baked Macaroni with Eggplant and Zucchini

Macaroni me Melitzanes ke Kilokithia Tou Fournou

Makes 6 servings

Soak diced eggplant according to the directions on page 78. Bring 6 cups water to a boil in a large saucepan and cook macaroni until just tender. Drain. In a large frying pan sauté eggplant and zucchini in olive oil until brown and drain.

Place macaroni in a buttered 9" x 13" baking dish. Evenly layer eggplant and zucchini over macaroni. Spread tomato sauce and top with mozzarella slices. Sprinkle parmesan cheese over all and bake in a 350° oven for 15-20 minutes.

Per Serving: Calories: 263, Protein: 14 gm., Fat: 12 gm., Carbohydrates: 17 gm.

½ lb. ziti macaroni

1 large eggplant, diced

1 large zucchini, diced

2-3 Tbsps. olive oil

1½ cups Tomato Sauce, page 67

½ lb. mozzarella cheese, cut in thin slices

¼ cup parmesan cheese, grated

Falafel

Falafel

Serves 6

2 cups dried chick
   peas,
   or 2 (16 oz.) cans
   chick peas

3 cloves garlic,
   minced

3 Tbsps. bread
   crumbs

½ cup parsley, finely
   chopped

½ tsp. cumin

salt and pepper to
   taste

½ cup flour

¾ cup oil for frying

6 Tbsps. Tahini Sauce,
   page 67,
   or Cucumber-Yogurt
   Salad, page 47

6 pita breads

shredded lettuce,
   diced cucumbers,
   tomatoes and
   peppers for garnish

If using dried chick peas, follow the directions for cooking chick peas in *Moussaka with Rice*, page 87, doubling the quantities indicated. Drain and rinse canned chick peas.

Mash the chick peas well with a fork, in the blender or food processor.

Mix in garlic, bread crumbs, parsley, cumin, salt and pepper. Chill for one hour. Make small balls, roll them lightly in flour. Heat oil in a small saucepan and fry falafel until golden. Transfer with a slotted spoon to paper towels to drain.

Cut the top of a pita bread, pour a little Tahini Sauce or Cucumber-Yogurt Salad inside the pocket, spread the vegetables and the falafel balls. Pour more sauce or salad on top and serve.

Per Serving: Calories: 330, Protein: 15 gm., Fat: 7 gm.,
   Carbohydrates: 50 gm.

Green Beans in Tomato Sauce
Fasolakia Yiachni
Makes 6 servings

From cities to villages in Greece green beans are cooked with onions, garlic and tomatoes and served as a maindish with a bowl of Rice Pilaf (see page 133). If you wish, you can add a few potatoes, cut in quarters and cook with the string beans.

Remove tips and strings from the green beans; wash and drain. In a 4 quart saucepan heat the oil and sauté the onions and garlic. Add tomato sauce and cook for a few minutes. Add string beans, parsley, oregano, salt and pepper, and stir. Add enough hot water to just cover, bring to a boil, lower heat and simmer for 45 minutes.

Serve warm or cold.

Per Serving: Calories: 91, Protein: 2 gm., Fat: 5 gm., Carbohydrates: 11 gm.

1 lb. fresh green beans or 2 (10 oz.) pkgs. frozen

2 Tbsps. olive oil

2 onions, chopped

1 clove garlic, minced

1 (8 oz) can tomato sauce

3 Tbsps. fresh parsley, chopped

½ tsp. oregano

salt and pepper to taste

hot water to cover

Humus
Revithia me Tahini
Serves 4

Tahini is usually used during fasting periods and in many Greek dishes. Besides being a main course, humus can be served as a hearty appetizer or a salad ingredient.

2 cups cooked chick
  peas (one 16 oz.
  can)

1 tsp. salt

juice of one lemon

½ cup tahini, diluted
  in ⅓ cup water

2 cloves garlic,
  minced

4 scallions, chopped

2 Tbsps. fresh
  parsley, chopped

If using dried chick peas, follow the directions for cooking chick peas in *Moussaka with Rice*, page 87. Drain, rinse and mash chick peas to a thick paste in a food mill or in a blender. Add remaining ingredients, beat well and chill.

To serve, scoop on lettuce, sprinkle with chopped parsley and tomato wedges. Or form into oblong balls and deep fry. Serve in pita bread with *Eggplant Tahini Dip*, page 54, and thinly sliced tomatoes.

*Per Serving: Calories: 221, Protein: 11 gm., Fat: 10 gm.,
  Carbohydrates: 22 gm.*

Tangy Humus

Revithia Poure me Skordo

Makes 4 to 6 servings

Mash the garlic and salt in a bowl with the back of a spoon. Add the chick peas and ½ cup water and mash vigorously to a smooth paste. Beat in the lemon juice, a few tablespoons at a time. Continue beating, pouring in the Sesame Dressing in a slow, thin stream until the mixture is smooth.

Per Serving: Calories: 260, Protein: 22 gm., Fat: 12 gm., Carbohydrates: 14 gm.

2 cups cooked chick peas (one 16 oz. can)

3 garlic cloves, finely chopped

1 tsp. salt

¼ cup lemon juice

1 cup Sesame Dressing, page 54

Herbed Lima Beans
Fasolia Yighantes Yachni
Serves 6

2 Tbsps. olive oil

2 onions, thinly
   sliced

2 cloves garlic,
   minced

1 (8 oz.) can tomato
   sauce

2 Tbsps. fresh
   parsley, chopped

½ tsp. oregano

½ tsp. salt

½ tsp. pepper

2 (20 oz.) packages
   large frozen lima
   beans

1 cup boiling water

Heat olive oil in an 8 quart pot and sauté onions and garlic. Stir in tomato sauce, parsley, oregano, salt and pepper. Bring to a boil. Add frozen lima beans and stir with a fork if necessary to break up.

When lima beans are well coated with the sauce and mixture boils again, add just enough water to cover them. Lower the heat, cover, and simmer for 20 minutes. Serve with a bowl of *Rice Pilaf* (see page 133) if you wish.

Per Serving: Calories: 187, Protein: 8 gm., Fat: 5 gm., Carbohydrates: 29 gm.

Lima Beans in Sour Cream
Fasolia Gigantes me Giaourti
Makes 4 servings

Cook the lima beans according to the package directions, then drain. While hot, add sour cream and scallions. Season to taste. Makes 4 servings.

Per Serving: Calories: 148, Protein: 6 gm., Fat: 4 gm., Carbohydrates: 17 gm.

1 (10 oz.) package frozen lima beans

½ cup sour cream, or ¼ cup yogurt and ¼ cup sour cream

3 fresh scallions, finely chopped

salt and pepper to taste

Baked Macaroni with Chick Peas
Pastitsio
Serves 12

Pastitsio is treat for the palate and the eye; it is a beautiful party dish. As with moussaka no English translation can express the taste of layers of macaroni and chick peas cooked in spices. It is topped with a thick sauce called bechamel, *since Greek cooking has been influenced by the French as well as by the Turks. This dish is a holiday favorite, and often served at large gathering. If my recipe makes more than you need, you'll find the dish just as good warmed up the next day.*

2 Tbsps. butter

1 large onion, chopped

2 (15 oz.) cans chick peas

2 tomatoes, peeled and thinly sliced

½ cup fresh parsley, chopped

1 tsp. cinnamon

½ tsp. pepper

1 cup parmesan cheese, grated

1 lb. large macaroni (preferably ziti)

SAUCE
6 Tbsps. butter
6 Tbsps. flour
4 cups warm milk
½ cup parmesan cheese (grated)

Melt 1 Tbsp. butter over medium heat and sauté the onion until soft. Mash half the chick peas and add to onions along with the remaining whole chick peas, tomatoes, parsley, cinnamon and pepper. Simmer covered for 5 minutes. Add ½ cup parmesan cheese, stir and let stand.

Cook macaroni in boiling salted water for 10 minutes. Drain well. Stir one tbsp. butter and another ½ cup parmesan cheese into the macaroni. Toss to combine.

To make the sauce, melt butter over low heat in a saucepan. Using a wire whisk stir in flour and blend well. Remove from heat. Gradually stir in milk, then return to heat and stir in vigorously until sauce is thick and smooth. Add the parmesan cheese, reserving some of the cheese to sprinkle on top of the pastitsio, and stir.

Place half the macaroni in a deep 9" x 13" baking pan and cover with the chick pea mixture. Layer the rest of the macaroni onto the mixture and cover with the sauce. With a spatula push some of the sauce around the inside of the pan and sprinkle with some of the parmesan cheese reserved from making the sauce. Bake in a preheated 350° oven until the top is golden and the sauce set, about 45 minutes. Remove from the oven and let stand 10 to 15 minutes before cutting.

Per Serving: Calories: 318, Protein: 17 gm., Fat: 15 gm., Carbohydrates: 21 gm.

Potato Patties
Patatokephtethes

Makes 16 medium-sized patties

This is a splendid accompaniment to vegetable dishes

Boil potatoes in a medium saucepan with just enough water to cover for about 40 minutes. Cool, slip skins or peel, and mash. Stir in egg or egg substitute, cheese and parsley. Mix well. Cover and refrigerate from 1 to 2 hours. With floured hands, shape potato mix into little balls. Roll them in flour, shaking off excess, and flatten. Add olive oil to a frying pan and heat until a drop of water landing in the oil sizzles. Fry potato patties until golden on both sides, adding more oil if desired.

*Per Patty: Calories: 144, Protein: 6 gm., Fat: 5 gm.,
    Carbohydrates: 17 gm.*

4 large potatoes

1 egg, beaten,
   or egg substitute

¾ cup kefalotyri or
   parmesan cheese,
   grated

2 Tbsps. fresh parsley, finely chopped

¾ cup flour

3 Tbsps. olive oil

Potato and Zucchini Bake

Patates me Kolokithakia Tou Fournou

Makes 6 servings

4 medium potatoes

2 zucchini, 8" long

⅓ cup olive oil

salt and pepper to taste

2 onions, chopped

6 cloves garlic, minced

1 (16 oz.) can whole tomatoes, cut into small pieces

4 Tbsps. fresh parsley, chopped

½ cup parmesan cheese

½ cup bread crumbs

Wash potatoes and zucchini and cut both into thin, round slices. Fry them in half of the oil in a large frying pan and season with salt and pepper. Set aside. Sauté the onions and garlic in the remaining oil. Add the tomatoes, parsley, salt and pepper to taste. Cook for about 15 minutes.

Add half of the cheese and 1 Tbsp. bread crumbs. Oil a 9" x 13" baking pan and spread the potatoes and zucchini in layers. Finish with the sauce.

Sprinkle with remaining cheese and bread crumbs. Bake in a preheated oven at 375° for 35 minutes.

Per Serving: Calories: 216, Protein: 5 gm., Fat: 10 gm., Carbohydrates: 28 gm.

Baked Potatoes with Cheese
Psytes Patates me Tyri

Makes 4 servings

Scrub and oil each potato. Bake in 400° oven until soft, about 1 hour. Remove from oven and cut in half. Scoop potatoes into a mixing bowl, reserving the shells. Add salt, pepper, and garlic powder and mash well. Add half of parmesan cheese, and milk, if necessary to make the potato filling smooth. Mix thoroughly.

Refill potato shells and sprinkle with remaining grated cheese. Bake at 350° until brown, about 10-15 minutes. If desired, place a slice of cheese on each potato and return them to oven until cheese melts, about 10 minutes.

Per Serving: Calories: 267, Protein: 15 gm., Fat: 7 gm., Carbohydrates: 35 gm.

4 baking potatoes

olive oil for brushing potatoes

salt and pepper to taste

1 tsp. garlic powder

½ cup milk

¼ cup parmesan cheese, grated

8 slices cheese (any kind) (opt.)

Spinach Pie
Spanakopitta
Serves 12

Spinach Pie *is loved by everyone. Try as a delicious cold leftover the next day.*

3 lbs. fresh spinach, or 4 (10 oz.) packages frozen spinach (thawed)

salt

2 Tbsps. olive oil

2 large onions, chopped

2 bunches scallions, finely chopped (including 4" green tops)

½ cup fresh parsley, chopped

½ cup dill, chopped, or 3 Tbsps. dried dill

4 eggs or egg substitute

½ lb. feta cheese, crumbled

If using fresh spinach, remove and discard coarse stems. Wash leaves well. Sprinkle lightly with salt; stir to spread salt evenly. Let stand 10 minutes; rinse off salt, and with your hands, squeeze out excess water. Cut up spinach and place in a colander so that remaining moisture will drip out. It is important that spinach be dry. (If using frozen spinach, do not use salt but do squeeze leaves as dry as possible and place in a colander to drain.)

In the meantime, heat 2 Tbsps. olive oil in a medium frying pan and sauté the onions and scallions until soft but not brown. Add spinach, parsley and dill, and cook, stirring, until the spinach has wilted, about 2-3 minutes. Remove from heat, transfer to a bowl, and let cool.

Beat eggs or egg substitute lightly, add the cheeses and blend well.

Combine remaining olive oil with 2 Tbsps. melted butter. Grease a shallow 9" x 13" baking pan. Take 8 phyllo sheets from the package. Center 1 sheet in the baking pan and brush lightly with the oil-butter mixture. Stack the other seven sheets one by one on top of the first, brushing each with the mixture as you stack it. The sheets will extend up the sides of the pan. Pour in the spinach mixture and spread evenly. Fold overhanging sides and ends of phyllo over the filling to enclose it. Brush with oil-butter mixture.

Top with 8 more phyllo sheets, brushing each with the oil-butter mixture as you stack it in the pan. Tuck overhanging edges around the inside of the baking pan to seal in the filling. Using the point of a sharp knife, score the surface into 12 rectangles. Bake in a preheated 350° oven until golden, about 45 minutes.

Do not cut through scored lines until ready to serve. Serve warm, cooled to room temperature or chilled.

Per Serving: Calories: 215, Protein: 12 gm., Fat: 11 gm., Carbohydrates: 19 gm.

½ lb. ricotta or cottage cheese

2 Tbsps. olive oil

2 Tbsps. butter, melted

16 sheets phyllo pastry (about ½ lb.)

Stuffed Tomatoes with Eggplant
Ntomates Gemistes me Melitzanes

Makes 6 servings

12 large tomatoes

1 large eggplant

1 Tbsp. salt

**¼ cup olive oil
or butter**

1 onion, chopped

**WHITE SAUCE
  2 Tbsps. olive oil
  2 Tbsps. flour
  1 cup milk, hot
  1 cup parmesan
    cheese, grated
  ½ cup fresh pars
    ley, chopped**

½ cup bread crumbs

Cut a thin slice from the blossom end of each tomato and set aside. Scoop out the pulp, remove seeds and set pulp aside. Drain tomatoes cut-sides-down.

Cut the eggplant in thick slices, sprinkle with salt, cover with water and soak for about 15 minutes according to the directions on page 78. Rinse, squeeze out excess moisture and cut in small pieces.

In a medium frying pan sauté the onion in ¼ cup olive oil or butter, add eggplant and fry until golden.

Prepare a white sauce, placing 2 Tbsps. olive oil in a medium saucepan with 2 Tbsps. flour and stir with a wire whisk until well blended. Remove from heat. Gradually whisk in hot milk, then stir vigorously. Return to heat and cook, stirring constantly, until sauce is thick and smooth. Add the cheese and parsley. Mix with the eggplant and stuff the tomatoes.

Cover each tomato with the reserved slice and sprinkle with bread crumbs. Place tomatoes in a large size baking pan. Add the tomato pulp and bake in a preheated 350° oven for 35-40 minutes or until the tomatoes are soft.

Per Serving: Calories: 312, Protein: 11 gm., Fat: 17 gm., Carbohydrates: 26 gm.

Tomatoes with Feta Cheese
Tamates me Feta
Makes 4 servings

Cut the tomatoes in half. Sprinkle with cheese, oregano, salt and pepper, and broil until red on top. Serve immediately.

Per Serving: Calories: 108, Protein: 6 gm., Fat: 6 gm., Carbohydrates: 8 gm.

4 medium round, ripe tomatoes

½ cup feta cheese, crumbled

1 tsp. dry oregano

salt and pepper to taste

Stuffed Zucchini "Little Shoes"
Kolokithia "Papoutsakia"
Makes 4 servings

This recipe is very popular in the cities and villages of Greece. This dish is made with small zucchini so the end product looks like "little shoes."

See photograph on front cover.

8 small zucchini

1 Tbsp. butter or olive oil

2 scallions, finely chopped

1 tsp. paprika

4 tomatoes, skin and seeds removed, chopped

salt and pepper

SAUCE
  2 Tbsps. butter
  2 Tbsps. flour
  1½ cups hot milk
  8 Tbsps. parmesan cheese, grated
  ½ tsp. dry mustard

Wash the zucchini and trim each end. Do not peel. Place in a large saucepan, cover with water and cook for 15 minutes. Drain and rinse with cold water. Cut a 1" wide lengthwise slice from each zucchini, scoop out the pulp and chop it. Sauté the scallions in butter or oil until soft. Add chopped zucchini pulp, paprika, tomatoes, salt and pepper. Stir and cook for 3-4 minutes.

To make the sauce, melt the butter in a saucepan over low heat, stir in flour and blend well using a wire whisk, stirring constantly. Remove from heat. Gradually add hot milk, stirring constantly and vigorously, return to heat and cook until sauce is thick and smooth (about 3 minutes). Take from heat, add 2 Tbsps. cheese and mustard, and season to taste.

Arrange zucchini in an oiled 9" x 13" baking dish and fill each with the stuffing mixture. Spoon cheese sauce over the zucchini, sprinkle with the remaining cheese and bake in a preheated 425° oven for 15-20 minutes or until golden.

Per Serving: Calories: 312, Protein: 15 gm., Fat: 14 gm., Carbohydrates: 27 gm.

Zucchini Patties
Kolokithokephtethes
Makes 20 to 22 patties

Cut off and discard the zucchini stems. Cut each zucchini into thirds. Place in a saucepan with salted water and cook until soft. Drain in a colander until dry. Mash and set aside.

Heat butter and sauté onions until soft. In a mixing bowl combine onions, zucchini pulp, cheese, bread crumbs, eggs or substitute, parsley, salt and pepper, and mix thoroughly. Cover and place in the refrigerator for 1 hour.

Shape into patties. Dredge patties in flour and pat to remove excess. Pour oil into a medium frying pan and heat until a patty placed in it sizzles. Fry patties until golden on both sides.

Per Patty: Calories: 83, Protein: 3 gm., Fat: 4 gm., Carbohydrates: 5 gm.

4 medium zucchini

2 Tbsps. butter

2 onions, chopped

¾ cup kefalotyri or parmesan cheese, grated

1 cup bread crumbs

2 eggs or egg substitute

2 Tbsps. fresh parsley, finely chopped

salt and pepper to taste

½ cup flour

¼ cup olive oil

Side
Dishes

Artichoke Hearts with Butter
Anginares me Voutyro
Serves 5

If you are using fresh artichokes, clean and soak them as directed in *Golden Breaded Artichoke Hearts*, page 73. Rinse and drain hearts. Cut in half; place in saucepan with remaining ingredients. Cover and simmer for about 40 minutes.

Per Serving: Calories: 186, Protein: 6 gm., Fat: 10 gm., Carbohydrates: 22 gm.

10 fresh artichokes
 or 10 canned,
 or frozen and
 thawed, artichoke
 hearts

2 onions, chopped

¼ cup butter

2 Tbsps. fresh dill,
 chopped,
 or 2 Tbsps. dried
 dill

1 tsp. salt

¼ tsp. pepper

1 Tbsp. flour

1 cup boiling water

Artichokes with Peas

Anginares me Araka

Makes 4-6 servings

**10 artichokes,
or 2 pkgs. (10 oz.)
frozen artichoke
hearts (thawed)**

**1 bunch scallions,
cut in large pieces**

1 Tbsp. olive oil

**1 (8 oz.) can tomato
sauce**

**2 Tbsps. fresh
parsley, chopped**

**1 tsp. dried
marjoram or dill**

**salt and pepper to
taste**

**3 cups fresh peas,
or 1 (1 lb.) pkg.
frozen peas**

If you are using fresh artichokes, clean and soak them as in *Golden Breaded Artichoke Hearts*, page 73.

Sauté scallions in the olive oil until translucent. Add tomato sauce, parsley, marjoram or dill, salt and pepper. Stir for a few minutes. Add artichokes and fresh peas, and stir again until well coated with sauce. (If you're using frozen peas, add them about five minutes before the artichokes are done.) Add hot water to almost cover the vegetables. Bring to a boil, then simmer for about 30 minutes or until soft. Serve warm or cold.

*Per Serving: Calories: 234, Protein: 12 gm., Fat: 3 gm.,
    Carbohydrates: 44 gm.*

Artichokes with Rice

Anginares me Ryzi

Makes 4-6 servings

Clean artichokes by removing the leaves and choke, leaving only the hearts and a little stem. As you clean each of them, immerse them in a bowl with enough cold water to cover, the juice of 1-2 lemons and 2 Tbsps. flour. Let soak for 10 minutes.

In a 4 quart saucepan sauté the onion in the oil. Add scallions, dill, salt, pepper, the juice of ½ lemon, hot water and the artichokes and cook until tender.

With a slotted spoon remove the artichokes and keep them covered in a warm place. Add the tomato paste to onion sauce and add enough water to make 2½ cups liquid. Bring to a boil, add rice, lower the heat and cook for 25 minutes.

Serve on a platter surrounded with the artichokes and, if you wish, accompany with yogurt.

Per Serving: Calories: 230, Protein: 8 gm., Fat: 7 gm., Carbohydrates: 35 gm.

4 artichokes

juice of 1-2 lemons

2 Tbsps. flour

1 onion, chopped

2 Tbsps. olive oil

2-3 scallions

½ bunch dill, chopped, or 1 tsp. dried dill

salt and pepper to taste

juice of ½ lemon

1 cup of hot water

1 tsp. tomato paste

1 cup uncooked rice

1-1½ cups yogurt (opt.)

Spicy Shredded Cabbage
Lachana Yachni

Serves 4

1 medium cabbage
(about 2 pounds)

2 Tbsps. olive oil

2 onions, sliced

1 (8 oz.) can tomato
sauce

1 tsp. salt

¼ tsp pepper

1 small bay leaf

2 whole cloves

1 cup boiling water

Remove and discard core of cabbage (or better still, eat core raw). Shred cabbage. Drop into boiling water for 2 minutes, then drain.

In an 8 quart saucepan, heat olive oil and sauté onion until soft. Stir in tomato sauce, cabbage, salt and pepper, bay leaf and cloves. Cook, stirring, for 2 minutes. Add boiling water, cover and simmer for 35 minutes. Remove bay leaf and cloves before serving.

*Per Serving: Calories: 109, Protein: 2 gm., Fat: 7 gm.,
Carbohydrates: 11 gm.*

Braised Carrots
Carrota Plaki
Makes 4 servings

Boil the carrots in salted water for 5 minutes, then drain. Heat the oil in a saucepan and sauté the garlic and scallions for 5 minutes. Add carrots, oregano, salt and pepper, stir and simmer for 15 minutes.

Sprinkle with lemon juice and serve.

Per Serving: Calories: 152, Protein: 3 gm., Fat: 3 gm, Carbohydrates: 28 gm.

1 lb. carrots (about 5 medium), peeled and sliced

1 Tbsp. olive oil

1 clove garlic, minced

1 bunch scallions, sliced

½ tsp. dry oregano

salt and pepper to taste

1 Tbsp. lemon juice

Cauliflower Fritters
Kounoupidi Tighanitos
Serves 6

Cauliflower Fritters taste even better cold. No picnic basket is without them.

1 large cauliflower

1 Tbsp. fresh
parsley, chopped

2 Tbsps. wine
vinegar

1 cup flour

1 tsp. baking
powder

1 tsp. salt

½ cup milk

1 egg, beaten,
or egg substitute

2 Tbsps. butter,
melted or olive oil

olive oil for frying

Cut off and discard thick stem of cauliflower. Place remaining head in a large saucepan, cover and boil whole in salted water until tender, 20 to 30 minutes. Drain. Separate into very small flowerettes. Sprinkle with parsley and vinegar. Let stand for 10 to 15 minutes, then drain.

Combine flour with baking powder, salt, milk, egg and melted butter or oil. Fold the flowerettes into the batter. Pour olive oil into a frying pan to a depth of ¼ inch. Heat until a drop of water sizzles when it lands in the oil. Carefully drop tablespoonfuls of the mixture into the oil and fry until golden brown on both sides. They will look flat. Drain on paper towels and serve warm, or chill and serve cold.

Per Serving: Calories: 86, Protein: 4 gm., Fat: 5 gm., Carbohydrates: 6 gm.

Eggplants with Cinnamon
Melitzanes me Kanella

Serves 4

Cut off and discard leaves and stems of each eggplant. Slit unpeeled eggplants lengthwise up to ½ inch before each end, but do not cut all the way through. Soak eggplants according to the direction on page 78, but do not slice.

While they soak, heat olive oil in a wide 4 quart saucepan and sauté the garlic lightly. Stir in tomatoes, salt and pepper, and simmer for 15 minutes.

Rinse and drain the eggplants. Squeeze out excess moisture and pat dry. Pour enough olive oil into a frying pan to cover the bottom. Heat until a drop of water landing in it sizzles, and fry eggplants lightly on all sides. Add more oil if necessary. Transfer them to tomato sauce, in one layer if possible. Sprinkle with cinnamon, cover and cook slowly for 15 to 20 minutes.

*Per Serving: Calories: 74, Protein: 22 gm., Fat: 3 gm.,
    Carbohydrates: 8 gm.*

10 very small eggplants (3 to 4" long)

1 Tbsp. olive oil

5 garlic cloves, split in half

1 (16 oz) can tomatoes

1 tsp. salt

¼ tsp. pepper

olive oil for frying

1 tsp. cinnamon

Eggplant in Tomato Sauce
Melitzanes Yachni
Makes 4-6 servings

2 large eggplants

2 onions, chopped

2 Tbsps. olive oil or butter

salt and pepper to taste

1 (8 oz.) can tomato sauce

½ cup parsley, chopped

Cut the eggplant in thick round slices and soak according to the directions on page 78. In the meantime, sauté the onions in the olive oil or butter. Sprinkle with salt and pepper. Rinse the eggplant and squeeze dry. Add the onion and stir until golden. Add tomato sauce and parsley, and let them cook over low heat until soft.

Per Serving: Calories: 139, Protein: 4 gm., Fat: 5 gm., Carbohydrates: 20 gm.

Baked Eggplants
Melitzanes Tou Fournou
Makes 4-6 servings

Cut the eggplants in thick slices. Soak according to directions on page 78, then rinse and squeeze dry. Lightly roll them in flour and fry in olive oil. Cut the tomatoes in thick round slices, remove the seeds (and the skins also if you wish) and fry lightly. Place the eggplant neatly in a baking dish, with the tomatoes on top, and sprinkle with chopped parsley, minced garlic and salt to taste. Top with bread crumbs and bake in a preheated 350° oven for about 15-20 minutes.

Per Serving: Calories: 298, Protein: 4 gm., Fat: 22 gm., Carbohydrates: 22 gm.

2 large eggplants

flour for rolling

½ cup olive oil

6 tomatoes

1 bunch parsley, chopped

2-3 cloves garlic, minced

½ cup bread crumbs

salt to taste

Stuffed Eggplants
Melitzanes Yemistes

Makes 4 servings

This is a lighter version of Stuffed "Little Shoes" *on page 88.*

4 small eggplants, 5-6" long

3 Tbsps. olive oil

1 Tbsp. butter

3 onions, chopped

2 cloves garlic, minced

4 tomatoes, peeled, seeded and chopped

½ cup fresh parsley, chopped

salt and pepper to taste

½ tsp. ground cinnamon

one bay leaf

Cut off and discard leaves and stem of each eggplant. Heat the olive oil in a large skillet, add the eggplant and cook over high heat until brown, turning on all sides. Remove from the skillet. Cut lengthwise in half and scoop out the pulp with a spoon, leaving a thin shell. Chop the pulp coarsely. Add the butter to the skillet and sauté the onions and garlic lightly. Add the tomatoes, eggplant pulp, parsley, salt, pepper, cinnamon and bay leaf. Cook for about 20 minutes. Remove bay leaf.

Fill the eggplant shells with this mixture and bake in a 350° oven for 15 minutes.

Per Serving: Calories: 255, Protein: 7 gm , Fat: 13 gm., Carbohydrates: 30 gm.

Whipped Eggplant
Melitzanes Poure

Makes 4 servings

Bake the eggplant in a 350° oven for 45 minutes. Remove from oven, let it cool and peel, discarding the skin. Chop in small pieces and whip in a blender until smooth, adding the milk, butter, salt and pepper. Serve warm.

Per Serving: Calories: 63, Protein: 2 gm., Fat: 4 gm., Carbohydrates: 6 gm.

1 large eggplant

½ cup milk, warmed

1 Tbsp. butter

salt and pepper to taste

Pie of Greens and Herbs

Hortopitta

Serves 15-20

2 lbs. fresh spinach, dandelions, chicory, endive or other greens

½ cup olive oil

1 bunch scallions (including green tops), chopped

½ cup parsley, chopped

½ cup fresh dill, chopped

½ tsp. cinnamon

salt and pepper to taste

⅔ cup cooked rice

20 sheets phyllo pastry (about ½ lb.)

Wash the greens very thoroughly. Dip all of the greens in a large pot of boiling water to wilt, then drain. Cut into very small pieces. Sauté the scallions in half of the oil. Add the greens, parsley, dill, cinnamon, salt, pepper and rice. Cook for 20 minutes. Cool.

With a little of the remaining oil, grease a shallow 9" x 13" baking pan. Take 10 phyllo sheets from the package. Center 1 sheet in the baking pan and brush lightly with oil. Layer the other 9 sheets one by one on top of the first, brushing each lightly with oil as you layer it. The sheets will extend up the sides of the pan. Place the greens on the phyllo and spread evenly. Fold overhanging sides and ends of phyllo over the filling to enclose it and brush with oil. Top with the remaining 10 phyllo sheets, again brushing lightly with oil as you layer them in the pan. Tuck overhanging edges around the inside of the pan to seal the filling.

Using the point of a sharp knife, score the surface into 20 rectangles. Bake in a preheated 350° oven until golden, or about 45 minutes. Do not cut through the scored lines until ready to serve. Serve warm or cold.

Per Serving: Calories: 119, Protein: 3 gm, Fat: 7 gm., Carbohydrates: 13 gm.

Leeks with Rice
Prassa me Ryzi
Makes 4 servings

Leeks arrive at the end of winter, green and fresh. They can be prepared in many ways, stewed, baked or combined with rice as the following recipe demonstrates.

Cut the roots from the leeks. Strip away any soft leaves and discard all but 2" of the green tops. Wash thoroughly under cold water, spreading the leaves open to rid them of sand. Slice into 1" pieces and set aside.

In a large saucepan sauté the onions until soft. Stir in the flour and salt, cook for a minute, then add the hot water. Bring to boil. Add the rice and the leeks, and stir until well coated. Reduce the heat, cover and simmer for 30 minutes. Cool to room temperature and serve with the lemon wedges.

Per Serving: Calories: 162, Protein: 4 gm., Fat: 7 gm., Carbohydrates: 23 gm.

2 lbs. fresh leeks (about 8 cups, sliced)

2 Tbsps. olive oil

3 onions, finely chopped

1 tsp. flour

½ tsp. salt

½ cup hot water

3 Tbsps. uncooked rice

1 lemon, cut into wedges

Okra with Tomatoes

Bamies me Ntomates

Serves 4

1½ lbs. whole okra

½ cup wine vinegar

½ tsp. salt

2 Tbsps. olive oil

2 onions, thinly sliced

1 (16 oz.) can tomatoes

2 Tbsps. fresh parsley, chopped

½ tsp. dried dill

½ tsp. salt

¼ tsp. pepper

Carefully cut off and discard okra stems and the skin around the stems, but do not cut into the flesh. Okra must be whole, with the juice sealed in, or the dish becomes gluey. Place them in one layer in a flat dish, sprinkle with vinegar and salt, and let stand for ° hour.

Heat olive oil in a wide frying pan and sauté onions until soft. Add tomatoes, parsley, dill, salt and pepper. Simmer until tomatoes are very soft.

Rinse the okra, drain and place side by side in the tomato sauce. Invert a heatproof plate on the okra, press down, and add just enough water to cover the rim of the plate. Cover the entire pan and simmer until tender, about ½ hour. Serve with feta cheese and Greek bread.

Per Serving: Calories: 148, Protein: 4 gm., Fat: 7 gm., Carbohydrates: 20 gm.

Onion Stew
Stifatho
Makes 4 servings

Stifatho is one of the most aromatic Greek dishes. In order to keep in all the flavor the Greeks seal the lid of the pot with a paste made of flour and water and then simmer the food for hours. It fills the house with its rich aroma while cooking.

Peel onions, and with a sharp knife cut two criss-cross slashes on the root end of each onion. This will keep them whole while cooking. Parboil the onions in a large amount of water for 1 to 2 minutes; drain.

Heat the oil and sauté the onion slices until soft. Add tomato sauce, garlic, bay leaves, cinnamon stick, salt and pepper. Stir and cook for a few minutes. Add the small onions and stir. Bring to a boil, reduce the heat and simmer for 1 hour. Remove bay leaves, cinnamon stick, and garlic cloves. Serve with rice.

Per Serving: Calories: 197, Protein: 3 gm., Fat: 13 gm., Carbohydrates: 17 gm.

2 lbs. small white onions

¼ cup olive oil

1 large onion, sliced

1 (8 oz.) can tomato sauce

4 cloves garlic

2 small bay leaves

1 cinnamon stick

1 tsp. salt

½ tsp. pepper

Orzo Pilaf
Kritharaki Pilafi
Makes 4 servings

2 onions, chopped

1 Tbsp. butter

1 (8 oz.) can tomato sauce

salt and pepper to taste

1 bay leaf

4 cups hot water

1¼ cup orzo (see page 7)

¼ cup parmesan cheese, grated (opt.)

In a 2 quart saucepan sauté the onions in butter. Add tomato sauce, salt, pepper and bay leaf, then stir. Add water and bring to a boil. Add orzo and stir a few minutes until it starts to boil. Lower heat and simmer, stirring occasionally, for 25 minutes. Remove the bay leaf. Serve hot on a platter and sprinkle with grated cheese, if desired.

Per Serving: Calories: 94, Protein: 3 gm., Fat: 4 gm., Carbohydrates: 14 gm.

Minted Peas
Araka me Dyosmo
Serves 4 to 6

Boil the peas according to package directions. Drain well and add butter, parsley and mint. Serve warm as a side dish.

Per Serving: Calories: 67, Protein: 2 gm., Fat: 3 gm., Carbohydrates: 9 gm.

1 (20 oz.) pkg. frozen peas

1 Tbsp. butter

1 Tbsp. fresh parsley, chopped

1 tsp. mint

Peas with Carrots
Araka me Karrota
Makes 6 servings

Heat water in a large saucepan. Add frozen peas, remaining vegetables, salt and pepper. Cover and cook on low heat for 20 minutes.
Serve warm.

Per Serving: Calories: 96, Protein: 4 gm., Fat: 0 gm., Carbohydrates: 20 gm.

¼ cup water

2 (1 lb.) pkgs. frozen peas

3-4 medium carrots, cut in thin slices

1 head romaine lettuce, cut in small pieces

1 bunch scallions, chopped

salt and pepper to taste

Peas with Scallions
Arakas me Freska Kremythia

Serves 4

1 bunch of scallions,
   chopped

1 Tbsp. olive oil

1 (8 oz.) can tomato
   sauce

1 Tbsp. fresh dill
   or 1 tsp. dried dill

1 tsp. salt

½ tsp. pepper

2 (10 oz.) packages
   frozen peas
   or 4 lbs. fresh
   peas, shelled

1 cup boiling water

In an 8 quart saucepan sauté scallions in olive oil until soft. Stir in tomato sauce, dill, salt and pepper. Add peas and stir again. Pour in boiling water, cover and cook over medium heat for 25 minutes. (If using frozen peas, cook for only 10 minutes.)

Per Serving: Calories: 164, Protein: 7 gm., Fat: 4 gm.,
   Carbohydrates: 25 gm.

Mashed Peas
Araka Poure
Makes 4 servings

Boil the peas. Drain well and mash with a fork or in a blender. Place in a 6 quart saucepan and add the milk, salt and pepper. Cook for a few minutes, stirring constantly. If necessary, add more milk to thin. Stir in butter to melt and serve.

1 lb. frozen peas

¼ cup milk

salt and pepper to taste

1 Tbsp. butter

Per Serving: Calories: 112, Protein: 5 gm., Fat: 3 gm., Carbohydrates: 15 gm.

Potatoes with Oregano
Patates me Rigani
Makes 4 servings

Peel the potatoes and place in a steamer or on a rack in a deep saucepan with enough water to cover rack. Steam for 15 minutes. Heat the butter or oil in a skillet and brown the potatoes on all sides. Add the salt, pepper and oregano, and cover and steam over low heat until tender.

8-10 small potatoes

1 Tbsp. butter, or olive oil

salt and pepper to taste

½ tsp. dry oregano

Per Serving: Calories: 141, Protein: 3 gm., Fat: 3 gm., Carbohydrates: 26 gm.

Braised Potatoes
Patates Yiachni

Makes 4 servings

4 potatoes

1 Tbsp. olive oil

1 onion, chopped

2 cloves garlic, minced

1 (16 oz.) can tomatoes

3 Tbsps. fresh parsley, chopped

salt and pepper to taste

Peel the potatoes and cut in quarters. In a medium saucepan sauté the onion and garlic in olive oil until soft. Add the potatoes and stir well. Add the tomatoes, parsley, salt and pepper. Cover and simmer for 30 minutes or until the potatoes are soft and the sauce is thick.

Serve warm.

Per Serving: Calories: 208, Protein: 6 gm., Fat: 4 gm., Carbohydrates: 41 gm.

Mashed Potatoes with Celery
Patates Poure me Selino

Serves 6 as a side dish

Clean the celery and potatoes, and boil in a medium saucepan in enough lightly salted water to just cover. Drain and mash. Little by little add hot milk, salt, and pepper. The mixture should be thick.

Place in a buttered 2 quart baking dish, sprinkle with cheese, and bake in a preheated 400° oven for 15-20 minutes or until golden.

Per Serving: Calories: 91, Protein: 5 gm., Fat: 2 gm., Carbohydrates: 11 gm.

2-3 medium potatoes

1 bunch celery

½ cup hot milk

salt and pepper to taste

¼ cup cheese, grated

Potato Moussaka

Moussaka me Patates

Makes 6 servings

3-4 lbs. potatoes
  (about 8 medium)

4 onions, chopped

2 Tbsps. olive oil

1 (8 oz.) can tomato
  sauce

½ cup fresh parsley,
  chopped

1 tsp. dry mint

salt and pepper to
  taste

⅛ cup bread crumbs

Wash potatoes, place in a large saucepan, and boil with the skins on until barely soft. Cut into thick slices.

Sauté the onions in the oil until soft. Add tomato sauce, parsley, mint, salt and pepper, and cook for 10-15 minutes. Add bread crumbs to thicken the sauce, reserving 2 tablespoons of the crumbs for baking. Brush a 9" x 13" baking pan with oil, sprinkle a few bread crumbs over the bottom, and arrange the popatoes over them. Cover with the sauce, sprinkle the remaining bread crumbs on top, and bake in a preheated 350° oven for 30 minutes.

*Per Serving: Calories: 221, Protein: 6 gm., Fat: 5 gm.,
  Carbohydrates: 40 gm.*

Roasted Potatoes
Patates Tou Fournou
Makes 6 servings

Place the potatoes in a 9" x 13" baking dish with oil and seasonings. Pour the lemon juice over the potatoes and toss together. Bake, stirring occasionally, in a 350° oven for 1 hour or until tender.

Per Serving: Calories: 144, Protein: 3 gm., Fat: 5 gm., Carbohydrates: 24 gm.

6 large potatoes, peeled and cut into quarters

2 Tbsps. olive oil

salt and pepper to taste

1 tsp. oregano

2 tsps. fresh parsley, chopped

2 cloves garlic, chopped

juice of one lemon

Rice with Grapes
Ryzi me Staphylia

Serves 4

2 cups boiling water

1 cup uncooked rice

1 tsp. salt

4 tomatoes, peeled
and cut up

1 Tbsp. butter

2½ cups water or
vegetable broth

2 cups seedless
white grapes

Bring water to a boil in a medium saucepan. Add rice and salt, and let stand until cool, about ½ hour.

To peel tomatoes, drop in boiling water for 1 minute, then rinse under cold water. The skins should slip off easily. In a large saucepan melt butter, add tomatoes and cook for about ½ hour. Add water or broth and bring to a boil. (If you are using only water, add ½ teaspoon salt.) Drain rice, rinsing it if it is starchy, and add to the tomato mixture. Cover and simmer for 15 minutes, then remove from the heat. Remove the lid, cover with a towel, replace the lid and let stand for 15 to 20 minutes.

Quickly pack the rice into a 4-cup ring mold. Cover mold with a platter, invert and turn out. Fill center of rice ring with grapes and serve immediately.

*Per Serving. Calories: 145, Protein: 3 gm., Fat: 3 gm.,
Carbohydrates: 27 gm.*

Rice Pilaf
Ryzi Pilafi
Serves 4

In a 4 quart saucepan heat the butter over low heat. Add the rice and stir until all the grains are evenly coated, about 2-3 minutes. Add salt and pepper. Pour in the hot water and stir. Lower the heat and simmer for 25 minutes.

Per Serving: Calories: 220, Protein 2 gm., Fat: 12 gm., Carbohydrates: 25 gm.

4 Tbsps. butter

1 cup uncooked rice

2½ cups hot water

1 tsp. salt

white pepper to taste

Rice and Orzo Pilaf
Pilafi me Ryzi ke Kritharaki
Serves 4

In a medium saucepan melt butter and sauté onion lightly. Add rice and orzo and cook, stirring constantly, until all grains are well coated. Add water, salt and pepper, cover and simmer for 25 minutes.

Per Serving: Calories: 114, Protein: 2 gm., Fat: 3 gm., Carbohydrates: 19 gm.

1 Tbsp. butter

1 onion, chopped

¾ cup uncooked rice

¾ cup uncooked orzo (see page 7) or other small pasta

3 cups boiling water

1 tsp. salt

white pepper to taste

Rice and Peas
Ryzi me Araka
Makes 4-6 servings

1 Tbsp. olive oil

1 onion, finely
  chopped

1 cup uncooked rice

1 (16 oz.) pkg. frozen
  peas, or 2 cups
  shelled fresh peas

salt and pepper to
  taste

2½ cups hot water or
  vegetable broth

¼ cup parmesan
  cheese, grated
  (opt.)

Heat the oil in a medium-sized heavy saucepan. Sauté the onions until tender. Add the rice and stir until all grains are well coated. Add peas, salt and pepper (you may want to use less salt if you plan to use vegetable broth), and stir. Add hot water or broth, bring to a boil and cook over low heat for 25 minutes. Serve with the cheese sprinkled on top, if desired.

*Per Serving: Calories: 150, Protein: 5 gm., Fat: 3 gm.,
    Carbohydrates: 32 gm.*

Tomato Trahana

Follow the recipe for Trahana as directed on page 135, except omit the eggs and milk, substituting 4 cups tomato sauce and 2 tablespoons butter.

Sour Milk Pasta

Trahana

Makes 4 to 5 pounds

Trahana is a pasta made by the peasants of the Greek islands and villages. Like Italian pastas, the name cannot be translated. Trahana looks like coarse oatmeal but the taste is different and more delicious. When made in Greek households trahana is dried in the hot sun during the day and brought into the house at night. It is usually made in the summer and stored for the winter. Use it as you would rice—it's especially good in soups.

Trahana can be made with either sweet or sour milk. This recipe is made with milk which has been left outside of the refrigerator to sour naturally.

In a large bowl combine all ingredients, using just enough water to make a firm dough. If it is too sticky before you add water, add more flour. Mix thoroughly with your hands. Shape into balls the size of an egg and flatten with your hands to ¼ inch thick. Spread a clean cloth on a table where the trahana may dry undisturbed, and place the rounds of dough to dry for one day, turning them over once. Then break them in smaller pieces and let them dry another day. Repeat the process of breaking them up and letting them dry until the pieces are small enough so that with your palm of your hand you can push them through a wide-holed colander from the outside. The finished pieces will be larger than rice grains and have a rough texture, hard as pebbles. The process takes 3 to 4 days.

Store trahana in sealed containers in a dry place. It will keep for many months—which is good because the recipe makes a supply that will last you quite a while.

4 to 5 pounds flour

2 eggs, lightly beaten, or egg substitute

4 cups soured milk at room temperature or yogurt

1 tsp. salt

Per Ounce: Calories: 67, Protein: 2 gm., Fat: 0 gm.,
Carbohydrates: 12 gm.

Spinach with Rice
Spanakoryzo
Serves 4

This spinach is loved even by children when it is made with fragrant oregano and dill.

1 lb. fresh spinach

salt

1 Tbsp. olive oil

1 bunch scallions,
  chopped

¼ cup fresh dill,
  chopped, or 2 tsps.
  dried dill

1 tsp. oregano

1 cup uncooked rice

2½ cups hot water

1 tsp. salt

¼ tsp. pepper

one lemon cut in
  wedges

Remove and discard coarse stems of spinach. Wash leaves well. Sprinkle lightly with salt; stir to spread salt evenly. After 15 minutes rinse off salt and squeeze out excess moisture with your hands. Cut up spinach and place in a colander to drain.

Heat olive oil and sauté scallions until soft. Add dill and oregano, and stir. Add rice and stir until all grains are well coated. Add hot water, salt and pepper; bring to a boil, cover and simmer for 20 minutes. Place spinach on top of rice and let stand for 5 minutes to wilt. Mix rice and spinach, adding a little more water and cooking 5 minutes longer if the rice hasn't cooked sufficiently. Serve with lemon wedges.

Variation: If desired, reduce the water to 2 cups and add ¼ cup tomato sauce or 1 tsp. tomato paste diluted in ¼ cup water.

Per Serving: Calories: 130, Protein: 6 gm., Fat: 3 gm., Carbohydrates: 20 gm.

String Beans with Potatoes
Fasolakia me Patates
Makes 6 servings

Heat the oil an 8 quart saucepan. Add tomatoes, parsley and oregano or mint; stir. Add the string beans, stir to thaw and add enough hot water to cover. Place the potatoes in among the beans. Season, cover and simmer for 30-35 minutes.

Per Serving: Calories: 122, Protein: 3 gm., Fat: 3 gm., Carbohydrates: 20 gm.

1 Tbsp. olive oil

1 (16 oz.) can tomatoes

2 Tbsps. fresh parsley, chopped

½ tsp. oregano or mint

2 (10 oz.) packages frozen string beans

1 large potato, cut in sixths lengthwise

salt and pepper to taste

Spinach Sauté
Spanaki Sauté
Makes 4-5 servings

If you use fresh spinach, wilt it first as follows: Put it in a pan without water, cover and cook over medium heat for about 5 minutes, removing the lid several times to check. Thaw frozen spinach.

In a medium saucepan sauté scallions in the olive oil or butter, add the spinach, dill, salt and pepper, and cook until done, about 20 minutes.

Per Serving: Calories: 72, Protein: 5 gm., Fat: 3 gm., Carbohydrates: 8 gm.

2 lbs. fresh spinach or 2 (10 oz.) pkgs. frozen spinach

1 Tbsp. olive oil or butter

1 bunch scallions, cut in small pieces

1 tsp. dried dill

salt and pepper to taste

Baked Tomatoes
Ntomates Tou Fournou

Makes 6 servings

3 large tomatoes

salt and pepper to taste

1 tsp. oregano

1 Tbsp. olive oil

4 cloves garlic, chopped

2 Tbsps. bread crumbs

¾ cup fresh parsley, chopped

Wash and dry the tomatoes. Cut in half. Place, cut side up, into a baking pan. Sprinkle with salt, pepper, oregano, and olive oil. Bake in a 400° oven for 15 minutes. Mix the bread crumbs with garlic and parsley. Remove the tomatoes from the oven, sprinkle each with the bread crumb mixture and broil for 5 minutes more, or until golden.

Per Serving: Calories: 73, Protein: 2 gm., Fat: 2 gm., Carbohydrates: 16 gm.

Tomatoes Baked with Herbs
Ntomates Plaki

Makes 6 servings

1½ lbs. tomatoes

4 medium onions, thinly sliced

1 bunch parsley, chopped

1 Tbsp. dill

¾ tsp. thyme

salt and pepper to taste

1 Tbsp. olive oil

juice of ½ lemon

Scald, peel and thickly slice the tomatoes. Place the tomatoes, onions, parsley, dill, thyme, salt, pepper, oil and lemon juice in a 9" x 13" baking pan. Cover and bake in a 400° oven for 30 minutes.

Per Serving: Calories: 54, Protein: 2 gm., Fat: 2 gm., Carbohydrates: 7 gm.

Stuffed Tomatoes
Yemistes Ntomates Laderes
Serves 6-8

This is the most popular stuffed vegetable in Greece. As with most vegetables cooked in olive oil, Stuffed Tomatoes,are delicious eaten cold, especially with some feta cheese and olives on the side.

See photograph on cover.

Cut a thin slice from the blossom end of each tomato and set aside. Scoop out the pulp, remove seeds and set the pulp aside. Sprinkle the inside of the shells with salt and drain, cut-sides-down.

Heat 1 Tbsp. olive oil in a large skillet and sauté onions and garlic until soft. Stir in half of the tomato pulp. Add the rice, boiling water, parsley, mint, cinnamon, salt and pepper. Simmer until all the liquid is absorbed. Stir in the raisins.

Stuff the tomatoes with the rice mixture. Top each stuffed tomato with the reserved tomato slice. Brush with olive oil and sprinkle with bread crumbs. Place tomatoes close together in a baking pan small enough and with high enough sides to support them. Add the remaining tomato pulp and ½ cup water. Place potato quarters between the tomatoes to help keep them upright. Bake in a preheated 350° oven until tomatoes are soft, about 1 to 1½ hours. Serve immediately or chill and serve cold.

Per Serving: Calories: 275, Protein: 7 gm., Fat: 3 gm., Carbohydrates: 57 gm.

12 to 15 large ripe tomatoes

salt

1 Tbsp. olive oil

4 medium onions, thinly sliced

4 cloves garlic, chopped

1 cup uncooked rice

1 cup boiling water

1 cup fresh parsley, chopped

1 tsp. dried mint

1 tsp. cinnamon

1 tsp. salt

½ tsp. pepper

1 cup black raisins

olive oil for brushing tomatoes

½ cup bread crumbs

½ cup water

2 potatoes, cut into quarters lengthwise

Cracked Wheat
Pligouri

Serves 4

1 Tbsp. butter

1 onion, chopped

1 cup cracked wheat

3 cups boiling water

3 Tbsps. soy sauce

In a medium-sized heavy frying pan heat butter and sauté onion. Add cracked wheat and sauté until golden and toasted. Add hot waterand soy sauce and simmer gently until the liquid has been absorbed, about 15 minutes. The cooking time will increase with the coarseness of the wheat.

Variation: Just before serving Cracked Wheat *sauté a handful of chopped walnuts in 1 Tbsp. melted butter until golden. Stir into the hot cracked wheat.*

*Per Serving: Calories: 157, Protein: 10 gm., Fat: 6 gm.,
    Carbohydrates: 19 gm.*

Zucchini au Gratin
Kolokithia o Gratin
Makes 4-6 servings

Wash zucchini, remove the tips and cut into thin slices. Dip in flour, shake and fry in 2 Tbsps. olive oil in a medium frying pan.

Make a white sauce by melting 1½ Tbsps. oil in a small saucepan and whisking in the flour. Take off heat and slowly whisk in the milk, stirring all the time. Return to moderate heat and stir until thick. Place a little white sauce and a layer of zucchini in a small (8" x 11") greased baking dish and sprinkle with a little cheese. Add another line of zucchini and sprinkling of cheese until all the zucchini and cheese is used. Pour the remaining white sauce on top, sprinkle with bread crumbs and bake in a preheated 350° oven for 15-20 minutes. Serve hot from the oven.

Per Serving: Calories: 234, Protein: 8 gm., Fat: 13 gm., Carbohydrates: 18 gm.

2 lbs. zucchini
(about 7 cups, sliced)

½ cup flour

2 Tbsps. olive oil

SAUCE
1½ Tbsps. flour
1 cup milk
¼ cup parmesan cheese, grated

½ cup bread crumbs

Zucchini with Garlic and Tomatoes
Kolokithia me Skortho kai Ntomates

Makes 4 servings

2 lbs. small zucchini
(about 7 cups,
diced)

1½ Tbsps. olive oil

2 cloves garlic,
minced

salt and pepper to
taste

1 (8 oz.) can tomato
sauce

¾ cup fresh parsley,
chopped

½ cup hot water

Wash the zucchini, trim each end and cut into small pieces. Sauté the garlic in olive oil in a large saucepan. Add zucchini and fry for 10 minutes. Add salt, pepper, tomato sauce, parsley and hot water, and cook over low heat for another 10 minutes. Serve.

Per Serving: Calories: 61, Protein: 1 gm., Fat: 5 gm., Carbohydrates: 8 gm.

Zucchini Pie
Kolokythopitta
Serves 12

Wash the zucchini. Using a vegetable scraper shred the zucchini. In a large heavy-bottomed saucepan sauté the scallions in 1 tablespoon of the olive oil. Add zucchini, parsley, nutmeg, curry powder, salt and pepper. Stir, cover and cook for 5 minutes. Add the rice, cover and cook for 15 minutes. If the rice is not soft at that time, add a little more water and cook until tender. The mixture should be dry, not watery.

Place the sheets of phyllo pastry in a 9" x 13" baking pan as in *Spinach Pie* (see page 100), using the remaining olive oil to brush the sheets. Bake in a 350° oven until golden, about 45 minutes.

Per Serving: Calories: 100, Protein: 2 gm., Fat: 5 gm.,
Carbohydrates: 13 gm.

2 lbs. zucchini (about 6 cups, shredded)

2 bunches scallions (tops removed)

¼ cup olive oil

1 bunch fresh parsley, chopped

1 tsp. nutmeg (optional)

1 tsp. curry powder

salt and pepper to taste

1 cup uncooked rice

10 sheets phyllo pastry (about ⅓ lb.)

Baked Vegetables
Briam
Makes 6 servings

1 lb. potatoes
(3 cups, sliced)

1 lb. zucchini (3½
cups, sliced)

1 lb. eggplant (about
4 cups, sliced)

1-2 green peppers

2 lbs. tomatoes

salt and pepper to
taste

2 onions, thinly
sliced

2 cloves garlic, thinly
sliced

½ bunch parsley,
chopped

¼ cup hot water

Peel and wash the potatoes (if you wish, leave the skin on). Slice them into thin rounds. Do the same with the zucchini, eggplants and peppers. Wash and peel the tomatoes and cut into thin slices. Spread half of the tomatoes into a 9" x 12" baking pan and season with salt and pepper. Spread the potatoes, zucchini, eggplants and peppers. Season again. Spread the onion slices and sprinkle with garlic and parsley. Top with the remaining tomatoes and season, if desired. Pour the hot water over the surface and bake in a preheated 325° oven for 1½-2 hours.

Per Serving: Calories: 117, Protein: 5 gm., Fat: 0 gm., Carbohydrates: 26 gm.

Baked Vegetables
Tourlou

Serves 6 to 8

As with many Greek vegetable dishes, this one is served at room temperature rather than hot to bring out the flavor of the vegetables.

Carefully cut off and discard okra stems and the skin around the stems, but do not cut into the flesh. Place in one layer on a flat dish, sprinkle with vinegar and salt, and let stand for ½ hour. Cut half the tomatoes into small pieces, reserving the rest. Cut zucchini, potatoes and eggplant into rounds ½ inch thick and combine with cut-up tomatoes. Add onion, garlic, green pepper, parsley, salt and pepper. Rinse the okra, drain and add to the other vegetables.

Transfer mixture to a 9" x 12" baking pan. Cut the reserved whole tomatoes into thin slices and place on top. Pour in the hot water, cover and bake in a pre-heated 325° oven for 1½ hours. Serve at room temperature with feta cheese and Greek bread.

Per Serving: Calories: 144, Protein: 6 gm., Fat: 0 gm., Carbohydrates: 33 gm.

½ lb. whole okra

½ cup wine vinegar

½ tsp. salt

2 lbs. tomatoes, peeled and seeded (about 6 cups)

3 small zucchini

3 potatoes

1 small eggplant

4 onions, thinly sliced

4 cloves garlic, minced

1 green pepper, seeded and sliced

1 cup fresh parsley, chopped

2 tsps. salt

½ tsp. pepper

1¼ cups hot water

Bread

Corn Bread
Bobota

Serves 6 to 8

Warm olive oil in a small saucepan or microwave. Measure cornmeal into a medium mixing bowl and add olive oil, stirring well until the oil is absorbed.

Sift the baking powder with the flour and add to cornmeal mixture. Add the rest of the ingredients except the raisins and mix well to form a thick batter. Fold in the raisins. Turn into an oiled 8" x 8" baking pan and bake in a preheated 375° oven for 25 to 30 minutes.

Per Serving: Calories: 297, Protein: 6 gm., Fat: 10 gm., Carbohydrates: 46 gm.

¼ cup olive oil

1 cup yellow cornmeal

4 tsps. baking powder

1 cup flour

1 egg, slightly beaten, or egg substitute

¼ cup honey

½ tsp. salt

1 tsp. cinnamon

2 Tbsps. frozen orange juice concentrate

1 cup milk

½ cup golden raisins

Pita Bread
Pitta

Makes 24 pita breads

6 cups flour (half whole wheat)

1 Tbsp. yeast

½ cup lukewarm water

1 tsp. salt

¼ cup olive or vegetable oil

2 cups lukewarm water

Place flour in a large bowl and make an indentation in the center. Place yeast in this indentation and pour water over it to dissolve. Let stand for 5 to 10 minutes.

Add remaining ingredients, then the 2 cups water to the flour and mix well. Turn dough out on a lightly floured board. Knead 5 to 10 minutes until dough is elastic. Place dough in an oiled bowl and flip it over once so top is oiled. Cover with a damp cloth and allow to rise until double, about 1 hour. Punch dough down. Form into a long rope 2" in diameter. Cut into 24 two inch slices and shape into smooth balls. Dip in flour and flatten slightly. Cover with a moist cloth and let rise 30 minutes.

Preheat your oven to 500°; it must be this hot to puff the breads adequately. Press the balls into flat ¼ inch thick cakes. Place on a lightly floured board and roll out into slightly thinner rounds. Cover and allow to rise 30 minutes until light. Place on large unoiled cookie sheets far enough apart so that they're not touching. Bake 4 minutes until just starting to brown and they are puffed out. Store wrapped in cloth or in a tight fitting container until they are cool so they'll remain soft.

Per Pita: Calories: 120, Protein: 3 gm., Fat: 2 gm., Carbohydrates: 21 gm.

Easter Twists
Tsourekia

Makes 4 braided loaves

The unique taste of this recipe is due to "mahlepi," a Turkish spice which can not be substituted with anything else (see page 6).

In a small saucepan bring the milk to a boil. Pour it into a large mixing bowl and add the sugar, butter, mahlepi and salt. Let cool to lukewarm. Dissolve yeast in warm water and add to lukewarm milk. Beat 4 eggs and add to the milk mixture.

Gradually stir in flour with a wooden spoon until the batter becomes too thick to stir. Coat your hands with flour and work in the rest of the flour by hand until a soft, elastic dough forms.

Cover with waxed paper and a thick towel and let stand in a warm place free of drafts for 2 to 3 hours or until the dough doubles in bulk. Punch down dough and knead again.

Divide the dough into 12 balls about the size of oranges. Roll each ball on a board into a rope 1½" x 2" thick and 15"-20" long. Braid three ropes together to make a "twist." Pinch ends and tuck under.

Place on greased baking sheets and let rise until twists are doubled in bulk. Preheat the oven to 350°. Brush the twists with the remaining egg (well-beaten) and bake until tops are a deep chestnut color, about 30 minutes. Check after 15 minutes, and if the color is darkening too quickly, reduce heat to 275° and continue to bake for ½ hour.

Cool on the baking sheets for 10 minutes and then invert on racks to finish cooling. Store in covered containers or wrap and keep in the freezer.

1 cup milk

2 cups sugar or honey

½ lb. sweet butter

1 Tbsp. mahlepi powder

pinch of salt

2 packages active dry yeast

½ cup warm water

5 eggs or egg substitute

10 cups flour

Per Slice: Calories: 279, Protein: 5 gm., Fat: 5 gm., Carbohydrates: 53 gm.

Raisin Bread
Stafithopsomo
Makes 2 loaves

2 packages dry yeast

½ cup water

1 cup milk

1 Tbsp. sweet butter

pinch of salt

½ cup honey

2 eggs, beaten,
  or egg substitute

6 cups flour

½ tsp. cinnamon

1½ cups seedless
  raisins or currants

milk for brushing

Dissolve yeast in ½ cup of warm water. Place in a warm place to rise.

Scald the milk and pour into a small mixing bowl. Add butter, salt and honey, and cool to lukewarm. Add beaten eggs.

Put 4 cups flour in a large mixing bowl, pour in the yeast and the warm milk mixture and beat vigorously for 2-3 minutes. Cover and set aside to rise for ½ hour. This procedure will give the bread a fine texture.

After half an hour add the cinnamon, raisins or currants and remaining flour. Knead for about 5 minutes until dough is elastic and smooth. Cover and let rise until doubled in bulk, about 1 hour.

Shape into two loaves and place in oiled loaf pans. Let rise again for 1 hour. Brush with milk and bake in 375° oven for 1 hour.

Per Slice: Calories: 133, Protein: 3 gm., Fat: 1 gm.,
*   Carbohydrates: 28 gm.*

St. Basil's Bread

Vasilopitta

Makes 3 braids

The Greek housewife bakes this special cake once a year, to honor St. Basil on his name day, which is also New Year's Day. The cutting of the Vasilopitta is on New Year's Eve, and relatives and friends are invited. When the clock strikes midnight, the hostess turns off the lights and then turns them on again to mark the end of the old year and the beginning of the new. Then it is time to cut the Vasilopitta in which she has hidden a single gold coin. Whoever finds the coin in his slice - so custom says - will have good luck for the whole year. The first piece is cut in honor of the Virgin Mary, the second is for the father of the family and the third for the mother. The rest of the family is served and finally the guests. The piece cut for the Virgin Mary is given to a needy person in the neighborhood.

Heat milk to scalding in a medium saucepan. Remove from heat, add butter, honey, mahlepi and salt. Let cool to lukewarm. Dissolve yeast in warm water and add to lukewarm milk. Transfer to a large bowl. Gradually stir in flour and mix until a soft elastic dough forms. It should not be firm. Cover with waxed paper and a thick towel and let stand in a warm place free of drafts for 3 4 hours or until dough doubles in bulk. Punch down dough and knead.

Divide dough into 3 parts. Make a braid from each part and then circle the braid until the ends touch. Place in individual oiled 9" round baking pans. Let stand again in a warm place until dough rises to almost double, about 1½ hours.

Brush with a little butter and bake in a preheated 350° oven until top is a deep chestnut color, 45-60 minutes. Check every 15 minutes and if the color is darkening too quickly, reduce heat to 325°. Cool in the pans for 10 minutes and then invert on a rack to finish cooling.

3 cups milk

¼ cup butter

2 cups honey

2 Tbsps. mahlepi powder (see page 6)

pinch of salt

2-3 pkgs. dry yeast

½ cup warm water

9 cups unbleached flour

Per Slice: Calories: 218, Protein: 4 gm., Fat: 2 gm., Carbohydrates: 45 gm.

No-Yeast St. Basil's Cake

Vasilopitta

Makes one nine-inch cake

As with the yeast-dough Vasilopitta, slip a coin underneath the cake before you cut it for your family and guests.

1 cup sweet butter

1½ cups sugar or honey

4 eggs or egg substitute

1 cup milk

3 cups flour

4 tsps. baking powder

1 Tbsp. grated orange peel

blanched almonds

Cream butter with sugar or honey in a large mixing bowl until light and fluffy. Add eggs or egg substitute, one by one, beating constantly, then add milk. Sift flour with baking powder and blend slowly into the mixture. Add grated orange peel. Transfer the mixture to a well-greased 9" round baking pan, sprinkle with a little sugar and a few blanched almonds and bake in a preheated 350° oven until top is a deep chestnut color, about 45 minutes. Check every 15 minutes and if the color is darkening too quickly, reduce heat to 325°. Cool in the pan for 10 minutes and then invert on a rack to finish cooling.

Per Slice: Calories: 411, Protein: 6 gm., Fat: 12 gm., Carbohydrates: 57 gm.

Zucchini Bread
Kolokithopsomo
Makes 20 slices

In a large bowl beat eggs until foamy; gradually beat in oil and sugar or honey. Add grated zucchini, cinnamon and salt. Mix the baking soda and baking powder with the flour. Gradually add flour and blend well after each addition. Fold in the chopped walnuts, if used. Pour into 2 breadpans and bake in a preheated 350° oven for one hour or until a knife inserted in the center of the cake comes out dry. Cool bread in the pan for 10 to 15 minutes and then turn out on a rack to cool.

Per Slice: Calories: 337, Protein: 4 gm., Fat: 14 gm., Carbohydrates: 49 gm.

3 eggs or egg substitute

1 cup olive oil

2½ cups sugar or honey

2 cups raw unpeeled zucchini, grated

2 tsps. cinnamon

1 tsp. salt

1 tsp. baking soda

½ tsp. baking powder

3 cups flour

1 cup walnuts, chopped (opt.)

Greek Bread

Psomi

Makes 2 loaves

This recipe can easily be doubled to make four loaves.

1 package active dry yeast

¼ cup warm water

1 tsp. salt

2 cups warm water

6 cups flour

Combine the yeast in ¼ cup warm water and rest in a warm place for about 10 minutes.

Add the salt to the 2 cups of warm water. Put the flour in a very large bowl. Make a depression in the center and add the softened yeast and the warm salt water. Using your fingers mix quickly until a firm dough is formed, adding a little flour, if necessary, so the dough will be firm. Knead, fold and punch the dough for 10 to 20 minutes, until smooth, satiny and resilient. Place in a floured bowl, cover with a clean towel and set in a warm draft-free area (an oven with no pilot light or covered with a wool blanket).

Allow to rise until doubled in bulk (approximately 2 hours). Uncover the dough, punch down and place it on a floured board. Divide the dough into 2 parts and knead each part separately for a few minutes, then mold with the palms of your hands to form the shape of long logs. Place them in oiled breadpans and let rise until doubled again in the same draft-free area for about an hour.

Bake on the center rack of a 375° oven for 10 minutes, then reduce the heat to 350° and continue baking for another 30 to 35 minutes, or until the crust is golden chestnut color.

Remove the loaves from their pans to wire racks, quickly wiping the tops with water-damped fingers or towel (a Greek baker's trick for glaze). Or you may brush the tops with melted butter. Cool before slicing.

Per Slice: Calories: 75, Protein: 2 gm., Fat: 0 gm., Carbohydrates: 16 gm.

Sweets

Apple Cake
Milopitta

Serves 8

Cream butter and honey together in a large mixing bowl until light. Add eggs and beat well, then add apple puree and sifted dry ingredients. Beat until smooth. Fold in raisins.

Pour into a well-buttered 8" square cake pan. Bake in a 350° oven for about 50 minutes.

Per Slice: Calories: 450, Protein: 6 gm., Fat: 13 gm., Carbohydrates: 91 gm.

½ cup sweet butter

1½ cups honey

2 eggs, beaten or egg substitute

1 cup apple puree or apple sauce

2 cups flour

¼ tsp. salt

1 tsp. baking powder

1½ tsps. cinnamon

1½ tsps. ground cloves

1 cup raisins, chopped

Baked Apples with Honey Syrup
Mila Tou Fournou me Meli

Serves 4

4 medium cooking
    apples

¼ cup walnuts,
    chopped (opt.)

¼ cup golden raisins

1 tsp. honey

½ tsp. ground cinna-
    mon

¼ tsp. ground cloves

1 cup water

1 cup honey

1 tsp. lemon juice

1 cinnamon stick

whipped cream
    (opt.)

Core apples, being careful not to cut through bottom. Pare ½ inch at the stem end.

Combine raisins and walnuts, if used, and 1 tsp. honey with the ground cinnamon and ground cloves. Fill the center of the apples with this mixture. Place apples in an 8" x 8" baking pan.

In a small saucepan combine water, honey, lemon juice and cinnamon stick and bring to a boil. Simmer for 2 minutes. Remove cinnamon stick and pour syrup over apples. Bake in a preheated 375° oven until tender, about 45 minutes, basting occasionally with syrup from the pan.

Serve warm or cold. Accompany apples with whipped cream, if desired.

*Per Serving: Calories: 419, Protein: 3 gm , Fat: 4 gm ,
    Carbohydrates: 100 gm.*

Apricot-Cognac Cake
Pasta Flora
Makes 24 pieces

Sift flour with baking powder and salt. Place in a large mixing bowl and add honey, butter, eggs, cognac and lemon peel. Knead well to make a soft dough and refrigerate for ½ hour. Set aside one-third of the dough. Press the rest into a well-greased 8" x 8" baking pan so that the dough covers the bottom and sides of the pan evenly. Spread the marmalade over the dough.

Shape the rest of the dough into six "ropes" the thickness of a finger and lay them on the marmalade in a crisscross fashion, attaching the ends to the top edges of the bottom-crust dough. Bake in a preheated 350° oven until golden, about 45 minutes. Cool before cutting.

Per Piece: Calories: 166, Protein: 2 gm., Fat: 3 gm., Carbohydrates: 30 gm.

3 cups flour

1 tsp. baking powder

pinch of salt

½ cup honey

½ cup butter, melted

2 eggs
or egg substitute

¼ cup cognac

2 tsps. grated lemon peel

1½ cups apricot marmalade

Crisp Orange Biscuits
Koulourakia

Makes 18 to 20 biscuits

¾ cup butter

¾ cup honey

2 eggs
  or egg substitute

juice and grated peel
  of one large orange

3 cups flour

2 tsps. baking pow-
  der

pinch of salt

Cream honey with butter in a medium mixing bowl until light. Add eggs one by one and continue beating. Add orange juice and peel. Sift flour with baking powder and salt, and slowly add to the butter mixture. Knead well to make a soft dough, adding more flour if needed.

Break off pieces of dough the size of a large walnut, roll into ropes and shape into twists, rings, pretzels or wreaths. Place on baking sheets and bake in a preheated 350° oven until golden, about 20 minutes.

Per Biscuit: Calories: 186, Protein: 3 gm., Fat: 5 gm.,
    Carbohydrates: 26 gm.

Halvah

Halvas

Serves 6

Combine water, honey, cloves, cinnamon stick and lemon peel in a saucepan. Bring to a boil, lower heat and simmer for 1 minute.

In another 8 quart saucepan heat the oil and slowly stir in farina. Add almonds and pine nuts, and continue stirring so the farina does not burn. When it turns a light chestnut color (in about 10 minutes) remove from heat but keep stirring.

Quickly bring the syrup back to a boil (stirring the farina all the while). Slowly and carefully add the syrup to the farina (the mixture will bubble furiously) and cook for 1 minute, stirring constantly. Remove from heat, cover with a towel, and let stand for 30 minutes. Turn the mixture into a 2½ cup mold. When partially cool, unmold and sprinkle with cinnamon. Let cool thoroughly, slice and serve.

Or, instead of turning mixture into a mold, use a tablespoon and your hand to shape individual mounds of the mixture on a platter. Sprinkle partially cooled mounds with cinnamon. Let cool thoroughly.

Per Serving: Calories: 300, Protein: 2 gm., Fat: 10 gm.,
  Carbohydrates: 50 gm.

1½ cups water

1 cup honey

3 whole cloves

½ cinnamon stick

1 sliver of lemon peel, about 1" long

¼ cup olive or vegetable oil

¾ cup uncooked farina

¼ cup almonds, blanched and slivered

¼ cup pine nuts (opt.)

ground cinnamon

Baklava

Baklava

Makes 36 pieces

Paper thin pastry, nuts and spices, a honey syrup—that is baklava.
This is a very popular sweet in Greece at any time, and a must for holidays and special occasions like namedays, christenings and weddings.

4 cups walnuts

1 cup almonds, blanched (opt.)

1 tsp. ground cinnamon

½ tsp. ground cloves

½ cup sweet butter, melted and kept warm

1½ lbs. phyllo pastry

3 cups honey

3 cups water

6 whole cloves

1 cinnamon stick

1 slice orange or lemon

Chop half the walnuts coarsely and the other half finely. Chop the almonds coarsely, if used. Mix nuts with ground cinnamon and ground cloves. Brush an 11 ½" x 17" baking pan with melted butter. Take 15 sheets of phyllo from the package. Place 4 sheets one on top of the other in the baking pan, brushing only the top sheet with melted butter. Stack the other 11 sheets one by one on top of the fourth, brushing each with warm melted butter as you stack it. Now, start sprinkling the nuts, evenly, one or two handfuls at a time. Take 2 more phyllo sheets from the package. Place one sheet at a time on the nut mixture; brush each with warm melted butter. Sprinkle evenly with more nut mixture. Repeat this layering process until all nuts are used. Then layer the remaining phyllo sheets, brushing each with the warm butter, until you have used all the sheets.

Heat the remaining butter until it sizzles and pour over the top sheet. Spread to cover evenly. With your fingers, press around the inside of the pan to seal the edges of the phyllo sheets together. Using a sharp knife, cut across the width of the pan, making strips about 2" wide. Then cut diagonally to make diamond shapes. Place pan on top shelf of a preheated 350° oven and bake until a deep chestnut color, crisp and baked through, about one hour. Check after the first ½ hour to see if baklava is browning evenly; if not, rotate the pan.

Let cool.

While the baklava is cooling, combine honey, water, cloves, cinnamon stick and orange or lemon slice in a saucepan. Stir in vanilla and almond extract. When the baklava is cooled, remove cloves, cinnamon stick and fruit slices from hot syrup and pour over the baklava; the syrup will be absorbed. Let cool and serve. The flavor improves the next day.

Per Piece: Calories: 249, Protein: 5 gm., Fat: 9 gm.,
   Carbohydrates: 37 gm.

1 tsp. vanilla

½ tsp. almond extract

Custard-Filled Pastry

Galaktoboureko

Makes 20 to 25 pieces

This is a popular dessert. The marvelous custard filling makes this sweet pastry so refreshing. "Galacto" comes from galo, (milk in Greek) and "boureko," meaning "stuffed." These are delicious fresh, but may be stored in the refrigerator a day or two.

5 egg yolks
  or egg substitute

1 cup honey

1 cup uncooked fari-
na

3 Tbsps. cornstarch

pinch of salt

6 cups milk

½ lb. phyllo pastry

⅓ cup sweet butter,
  melted

1½ cups honey

1 cup water

4 whole cloves

1 cinnamon stick

1 thin slice of
  orange

1 tsp. vanilla

ground cinnamon

In a medium saucepan, beat egg yolks with the honey. Add the farina, cornstarch and salt, and blend well. Slowly pour in milk. Cook the mixture over low heat, stirring constantly, until it thickens. Remove from heat and let cool.

Take half the phyllo sheets (about 7) from the package. Center one sheet in a buttered 9" x 13" baking pan and brush with melted butter. Stack the other 6 sheets one by one on top of the first, brushing each with melted butter as you stack it. The sheets will extend up the sides of the pan. Spoon in the custard and spread evenly. Fold overhanging sides and ends of phyllo over the filling to enclose it. Brush with melted butter.

Cover with the remaining 7 phyllo sheets, brushing each with melted butter as you stack it in the pan. Trim overhanging edges and make additional layers with the trimmings, placing them under the topmost sheet of phyllo and brushing each with the butter. Using the point of a sharp knife, score the surface into diamond shapes. Be careful not to cut into the filling. Bake in preheated 350° oven until golden, about 45 minutes.

While the pastry is baking, combine 1½ cups honey, the water, whole cloves, cinnamon stick and orange slice in a saucepan and bring to a boil for 5 minutes. Remove from heat. Skim the froth; remove cloves, cinnamon stick and orange slice. Stir in vanilla. As soon as you remove the pastry from the oven pour this hot syrup over it; it will be absorbed.

Let cool thoroughly, cut through scored lines, sprinkle with cinnamon and serve. Store in the refrigerator.

Per Piece: Calories: 201, Protein: 3 gm., Fat: 3 gm.,
*   Carbohydrates: 41 gm*

Custard-Filled "Flutes"
Flogheres
Makes 26 to 28 "flutes"

In a medium saucepan beat egg yolks with ¼ cup of honey. Add farina and mix well. Slowly stir in hot milk and add lemon peel. Lower the heat and cook, stirring constantly, until thickened. Remove from heat and let cool.

Take 1 phyllo sheet and cut in half across the width of the sheet. Brush each half with melted butter and fold in half, bringing the end of the sheet together.

Place 1 tablespoon custard at a narrow end and fold long sides in toward the middle to enclose filling. Brush with melted butter and roll up into a tube shape or "flute." Repeat with other half-sheet. Place "flutes" in a large baking pan and brush with melted butter again. Repeat cutting, filling and rolling process with the remaining sheets. Bake in a preheated 350° oven until golden, about 25 minutes. Prick each "flute" with a fork and let cool.

While the "flutes" are cooling, combine 1½ cups honey and the water with lemon juice in a saucepan and bring to a boil. Simmer for 5 minutes. Skim the froth. Pour hot syrup over the partially cooled "flutes" and let them absorb it. Serve cool.

Per Flute: Calories: 105, Protein: 2 gm., Fat: 3 gm.,
*   Carbohydrates: 16 gm.*

3 egg yolks
  or egg substitute

¼ cup honey

½ cup uncooked
  farina

3 cups hot milk

1 sliver of lemon
  peel, about ½ inch
  long

½ lb. phyllo pastry

½ cup butter, melted

1½ cups honey

1 cup water

juice of ½ lemon

Grape Pudding
Moustalevria

Serves 4

In Greece, moustalevria is customarily made only once a year, during the wine harvest, when fresh grapes and must (unfermented juice) are available. The village and island people crush the grapes in a "patitiri," a round stone trough lined with flat stones. On some of the islands this wine press is called "linare," and in the villages of northern Greece, people call it "cavos." But no matter what it is called, every household in the islands and villages has to have a wine press.

Early in the morning on a harvest day everybody hangs huge willow baskets on the family's mules or donkeys. Then they all go to the vineyards to collect the grapes and load them into the baskets. Back home the grapes are turned out into the patitiri. The family members wash their feet and everybody jumps onto the grapes. Laughing and singing, they trample the grapes and the must (moustos) runs out of a spout into a large container. Before the must is transferred to wooden barrels for fermenting into wine, some is drained off to make moustalevria. In America, with different grape juices on the market, it is very easy to make this exotic dessert all year long.

3 Tbsps. sesame seeds

3 cups unsweetened grape juice

¼ cup cornstarch

6 Tbsps. honey

¼ cup nuts, chopped (opt.)

cinnamon

Toast the sesame seeds for 5 minutes in a preheated 325° oven. Set aside. Add ¼ cup grape juice to the cornstarch and set aside. In a saucepan combine the remaining grape juice and the honey and bring to a boil. Add the cornstarch mixture and cook, stirring constantly, until juice thickens. Pour into 4 individual bowls and let cool. Sprinkle with sesame seeds, nuts and cinnamon. Chill and serve cold.

Per Serving: Calories: 191, Protein: 2 gm., Fat: 1 gm., Carbohydrates: 38 gm.

Tart Grape Pudding
Moustalevria

Makes 6-8 servings

We do not use sugar at all in this recipe. It is not very sweet but it is very healthful.

Separate the grapes from the stems. Place in a large pot with enough water to cover them well and boil for 45 minutes. Drain. You should have about 7 cups of liquid. Place the grapes in a colander and press to remove all the juice. Add it to the cooking liquid. Add the farina and let boil, stirring occasionally, until thick.

Pour into individual bowls and let cool. Sprinkle with cinnamon and chopped walnuts and chill.

3-4 lbs. black grapes, or any kind of very sweet grapes

1 cup farina

cinnamon

chopped walnuts (opt.)

Per Serving: Calories: 45, Protein: 1 gm., Fat: 0 gm., Carbohydrates: 11 gm.

Greek Coffee

Kaffes

Serves 1

Greece's trademark is Greek coffee. In the sidewalk cafes every tourist visiting Greece sees coffee drinkers with their demitasse cups of thick coffee.
I'll tell you how to make Greek coffee just like the cafes do it. We call it Greek coffee although it has been ours for only 500 years—since the Turks introduced it to the Greeks in the fifteenth century.
Now, in the twentieth century, every household in Greece owns a "briki,"
the special coffee pot you need for this coffee.
Greek coffee is sold by the pound in Greek and Middle Eastern stores. Brikia (the coffee pots) can be found in the same stores, or you may find both in specialty food shops. This combination of the right coffee and the right pot is what makes Greek coffee so flavorful and strong. The coffee is brewed with or without sugar. It may be "sketos" (straight without sugar), "metrios" (medium sweet), "glykos" (sweet) or "varys glykos" (very sweet). The following recipe is "metrios."

1 tsp. Greek coffee

1 tsp. sugar

1 demitasse cup water

Increase the amount of sugar if you prefer. The amount of each ingredient may be increased proportionately if you want to serve more than one demitasse cup at a time.

Place coffee and sugar in a "briki" and blend. Add the water, stir well and bring to a boil.

As soon as the coffee reaches the rim of the "briki" lift the pot from the heat and pour a little of the foam into the cup. This is very important as the "kaimaki" (cream of the coffee) is the foam formed by the first boil. Return the "briki" to the heat and allow the coffee to boil to the rim again. Pour the coffee into the cup, being very careful not to disturb the "kaimaki." Let coffee stand a few seconds before sipping, so that the grounds may settle.

Per Serving: Calories: 14, Protein: 0, Fat: 0,
Carbohydrates: 4 gm.

Spiced Honey Cakes
Melomakarona (or) Phoenikia

Makes 15 to 20 cakes

The ancient Phoenicians brought to the Greek islands their language and these spicy cakes. In Greece today, mostly on the islands, melomakarona are baked for New Year's Day. For a festive look, before they go into the oven each cake is pressed with the bottom of a cut-glass dish or with a special wooden seal and then baked, decorated-side-up.

Mix flour with baking powder and baking soda and set aside. Beat olive oil with orange juice, cinnamon, ground cloves and salt and continue beating. Gradually stir in flour and mix well until a medium soft dough is formed. Let stand for 10 to 15 minutes. Start the oven now, setting it to 350°. Shape dough into mounded ovals, the size of a large walnut and flat on the bottom. Place on an ungreased baking sheet and bake until light golden, about 20-25 minutes. Let cool.

While the honey cakes are cooling, combine all syrup ingredients except almond extract in a large saucepan. Bring to a boil for 5 minutes. Skim the froth and remove the cloves, cinnamon stick and orange slice and add the almond extract. With a slotted spoon, dip the cooled honey cakes into the hot syrup for 30 to 35 seconds. Remove carefully and place on a platter. Combine topping ingredients and sprinkle on each cake.

Per Cake: Calories: 278, Protein: 3 gm., Fat: 16 gm., Carbohydrates: 30 gm.

1 cup whole wheat flour

1 cup + 2 Tbsps. white flour

1 tsp. baking powder

½ tsp. baking soda

1 cup olive oil

¾ cup orange juice

1 tsp. cinnamon

½ tsp. ground cloves

pinch of salt

SYRUP
1 cup honey
1 cup water
5 whole cloves
1 cinnamon stick
1 thin orange slice
½ tsp. almond extract

TOPPING
1 cup walnuts, finely chopped
½ tsp. cinnamon
½ tsp. ground cloves

Baked Shredded Wheat Pastry
Katayifi

Makes 20 to 25 pieces

The katayiki, shredded wheat pastry dough, can be found in 1 lb. packages in Greek or Middle Eastern food stores. Katayiki is another form of phyllo dough used in baklava. It is shredded and packed in bags rather than in boxes like phyllo. Keep it in the freezer until the day it is to be used. Defrost in its container to room temperature.

2 cups walnuts or blanched almonds, finely chopped

1 tsp. ground cinnamon

½ cup orange juice

2 lbs. katayiki dough (see page 7)

½ cup sweet butter, melted

SYRUP
  2 cups honey
  2 cups water
  6 whole cloves
  1 cinnamon stick
  1 thin slice orange

In a bowl mix walnuts or almonds with cinnamon and orange juice. Take the shredded wheat out of its packaging and open it on a table for 10-15 minutes. Spread half of it on a greased 9" x 12" baking pan and brush with half of the butter. Spread the walnut or almond mixture over it and cover with remaining pastry. Brush with the remaining butter and bake in a moderate oven (350°) for 45 minutes or until golden on top.

For the syrup boil honey, water, cloves, cinnamon and orange slice for 7-10 minutes. Keep hot; when the katayiki is done remove the cloves, cinnamon stick and orange slice, and spoon the syrup over the surface. Cover the pan with a clean Turkish towel to trap the steam and make it soft. When cool, cut into diamond or square shapes of any size. Cool and serve.

Note: Instead of using nuts for the filling, you can use custard as in Galaktoboureko, page 166. Use half of the amount.

Per Piece: Calories: 309, Protein: 6 gms., Fat: 12 gm., Carbohydrates: 51 gm.

Shredded Pastry Rolls
Katayifi

Makes 30 to 35 rolls

Mix walnuts or almonds with honey, bread crumbs and cinnamon. With buttered hands pick up a small amount of katayiki dough. Place one tablespoon of the nut mixture at one end of the handful of dough, seal the filling by covering it with part of the dough and shape roll into an oval that just fits into your palm. Repeat with remaining dough and filling. Place rolls neatly in a buttered 9" x 13" baking pan and pour melted butter over the top. Bake in a preheated 325° oven until light golden, about 40 minutes.

While rolls are baking, make a syrup by combining honey, water and the orange slice in a saucepan. Bring to a boil, lower the heat and simmer for 7-10 minutes. Skim the froth, remove from heat and stir in vanilla. As soon as you remove the rolls from the oven, pour hot syrup over them. Cover the pan so the steam will make the rolls soft. Then let cool and serve.

Per Roll: Calories: 260, Protein: 6 gm., Fat: 11 gm., Carbohydrates: 37 gm.

4 cups walnuts or blanched almonds, chopped

½ cup honey

2 Tbsps. bread crumbs

1 Tbsp. cinnamon

2 lbs. katayiki dough (see page 7)

½ cups sweet butter, melted

SYRUP
3 cups honey
3 cups water
1 thin slice orange
1 tsp. vanilla

Honey-Cheese Cake
Melopitta
Makes about 10-12 pieces

Melopita is a popular traditional dessert throughout the islands of Greece. The taste is derived from honey (meli in Greek). The islanders prepare and enjoy it during their Easter celebration.

2 cups flour

½ tsp. baking soda

¼ tsp. salt

½ cup cold butter

¼ cup milk

1 lb. fresh unsalted mizithra, ricotta or farmer's cheese

½ cup honey

¼ tsp. salt

½ cup milk

½ cup honey

1 tsp. cinnamon or grated peel of one lemon

4 eggs, well beaten, or egg substitute

approx. 3 Tbsps. cinnamon

Sift flour into a medium mixing bowl with baking powder and ¼ tsp. salt. Cut cold butter into flour mixture until it is evenly distributed. Stir in milk and form mixture into a ball. Cover and place in refrigerator for ½ hour. While pastry is chilling combine cheese, honey, salt, milk, the honey and cinnamon or lemon peel. Add eggs, mix thoroughly and set aside.

Roll out pastry one eighth inch thick. Press into either an 8" x 11" x 2" baking pan or a 10" round baking pan, letting the extra extend up the sides of the pan. Pour filling onto pastry dough. Bake in a preheated 350° oven for one hour. Sprinkle generously with additional cinnamon. Let cool.

Using a sharp knife, cut across the width of the pan, making strips about 2 inches wide. Then make diagonal cuts 2 inches apart so that pieces are diamond-shaped.

Per Piece: Calories: 322, Protein: 9 gm., Fat: 9 gm., Carbohydrates: 42 gm.

Honey Puffs
Loukoumathes
Makes about 70

In tiny neighborhood shops all over Greece, from the seacoast towns to Athens itself, you will still see bakers frying these in huge pots full of boiling oil. The puffs are sold steaming hot and eaten on the spot. But first the baker pours on warm honey, followed by a sprinkling of cinnamon and sometimes by chopped walnuts. In my home loukoumathes are the family's favorite Sunday breakfast.

Sift flour into a bowl and make a well in the center.

Dissolve yeast and salt in warm water. Pour mixture into the well and combine. Add 1 cup water to make a thick batter, using more if necessary. Cover and let stand in a warm place for 1-2 hours.

Pour oil into a heavy saucepan to a depth of 4 inches, and heat oil to just before the smoking point. Drop the batter by tablespoonfuls into the hot oil four at a time. Using tongs turn puffs until a ruddy chestnut color on all sides. Remove, drain on paper towels and serve hot with honey, cinnamon and nuts.

Hint: *If you are in a hurry, use commercial unbaked biscuits which come in tubes. Cut them in four pieces and fry as above.*

If the oil hasn't gotten hot enough to smoke while being used, it may be strained, refrigerated and used several times before discarding.

6 cups flour

1 package active dry yeast

pinch of salt

1 cup warm water

olive or vegetable oil for frying

honey

cinnamon

chopped walnuts (opt.)

Per Puff: Calories: 39, Protein: 1 gm., Fat: 3 gm., Carbohydrates: 9 gm.

Quick Honey Puffs
Loukoumathes

Makes about 3 dozen

This is an easier version than the recipe on page 175. You do not have to wait for the yeast to rise as you use sour cream and baking powder instead and fry them immediately.

1 (16 oz.) container
   sour cream

2 tsps. baking pow-
   der

2 cups flour

2 cups milk

2 eggs
   or egg substitute

honey and cinna-
   mon

chopped nuts (opt.)

Combine above ingredients and mix well. If batter is too soft, add more flour. (It should look like thick pancake batter.) Drop a tablespoon of dough into hot oil and fry until golden. Using tongs, remove and drain puffs, and serve with honey, cinnamon and nuts.
Sprinkle with honey and cinnamon and serve hot.

Per Puff: Calories: 104, Protein: 2 gm., Fat: 5 gm., Carbohydrates: 10 gm.

Rice Pudding
Ryzogalo
Serves 6

Ryzogalo is very traditional in Greece and means "rice-milk."
This dessert is made by every household as well as the public cafes.

In a heavy saucepan bring water and salt to a boil. Add rice, lower heat, cover and simmer for 5 minutes or until all the water is absorbed.

Heat milk and add to rice along with lemon peel. Bring to a boil, lower heat and cook, stirring frequently, for 30 minutes. Add honey and cook 15 minutes more. Dissolve cornstarch in water and stir into the pudding. Cook for 5 minutes. Remove from heat. Discard the lemon peel; stir in vanilla and almond extract. The pudding will not look very thick, but it thickens as it cools. Pour into 6 individual dishes. Let cool to room temperature and sprinkle with cinnamon. Cover with plastic wrap and refrigerate. Serve cold.

Per Serving: Calories: 274, Protein: 6 gm., Fat: 4 gm.,
Carbohydrates: 51 gm.

1 cup water

pinch of salt

⅔ cup rice

1 quart milk

1" sliver of lemon peel

¾ cup honey

3 tsps. cornstarch

3 tsps. water

1 tsp. vanilla

½ tsp. almond extract

cinnamon

Semolina Cake
Serves 12

*Semolina is a very finely ground wheat flour, with a low starch content.
Like farina it is found in the Greek, Italian or Syrian stores.
If you cannot find it, use farina which you can find in any supermarket.*

3 cups yellow semolina

2 cups honey

½ to ¾ cups cold water

¾ cup melted unsalted butter

20 whole blanched almonds, split in half lengthwise

SYRUP
1 cup honey
1½ cup water
2 Tbsps. lemon juice
½ tsp. rose water (opt.)

In a large mixing bowl combine semolina, honey, water and mix well. Add melted butter, a teaspoon at a time, and beat vigorously until it is completely absorbed. Pour the batter into a well greased 8" x 12" baking pan, spreading it evenly. Score the top into diamond shapes, place an almond half on each diamond and bake in a preheated 350° oven for 1 hour or until the cake is firm to the touch.

Make the syrup by combining the water, honey and the juice in a small saucepan. Bring to a boil (watching that it doesn't boil over), lower heat and simmer for 5 minutes.

When the cake is done pour the hot syrup over it and let it cool.

*Per Serving: Calories: 397, Protein: 2 gm., Fat: 13 gm.,
Carbohydrates: 76 gm.*

Deep-Fried Twists
Diples (or) Xerotigana
Makes about 3 dozen

This is a traditional sweet for festive occasions. Before you drop the strips into oil to fry, you can create different shapes, such as bows and twists. Use your imagination!

In a saucepan make a syrup by combining the honey, water and orange slice. Bring to a boil, lower the heat and simmer for 5 minutes. Keep warm.

Stir baking soda and salt into the orange juice. Mix olive oil, orange juice mixture and flour to form a soft dough. Knead until dough is elastic and smooth, adding more flour if necessary. Divide into 3 balls. Flour a large board, and roll each ball with a rolling pin into a circle one third inch thick. Using a sharp knife, cut into 2" x 4" strips. Cover until ready to fry.

Heat 4 inches of oil in a heavy saucepan until hot. Drop strips one at a time into the hot oil. They will bubble immediately. Use two forks to twist and turn each strip, frying to an even golden color. Remove carefully and set on a paper towel to drain. Serve them with the warm syrup. Dust with cinnamon and serve them with warm syrup.

2 cups honey

2 cups water

1 thin slice orange

1 tsp. baking soda

pinch of salt

2 cups orange juice

½ cup olive
or vegetable oil

3½ cups flour

oil for frying

cinnamon

*Per Twist: Calories: 128, Protein: 1 gm., Fat: 3 gm.,
Carbohydrates: 25 gm.*

Honey Soaked Pastry Wheels
Rothelles (or) Saraili

Makes 20 to 25 wheels

The word "rothelles" comes from the Greek word for "wheel." Someone thought the spiral of fill-ing in each pastry slice looked like a wheel in motion. These taste similar to baklava.

4 cups walnuts, chopped

1 Tbsp. cinnamon

1 tsp. ground cloves

1 lb. phyllo pastry

½ cup sweet butter, melted

SYRUP
2 cups honey
2 cups water
1 thin slice orange
6 whole cloves
1 cinnamon stick
1 tsp. vanilla
cinnamon to sprinkle

Mix nuts, cinnamon and ground cloves. Spread the phyllo on the table and cover with a damp towel to keep it from drying. Take 2 phyllo sheets and brush one lightly with butter. Place the second sheet on top of the first and brush with melted butter. Sprinkle evenly with a handful of the nut mixture. Roll it jelly-roll fashion and place on an 11" x 17" buttered baking sheet. Repeat the same process and place neatly in the pan until you finish with all ingredients. Pour any remaining warm butter on top of the rolls and cut them into 4" lengths. Score tops in several places. Bake in a preheated 350° oven for about 25 minutes or until golden brown.

While the rolls are cooling, make a syrup by combining honey, water, the orange slice, the cloves and cinnamon stick in a saucepan. Bring to a boil and simmer for 5 minutes, skimming off the froth that forms. Remove from heat, remove whole cloves, orange slice, and cinnamon stick. Stir in vanilla. Pour the syrup over the rolls. Let cool thoroughly, cut through the scored lines, sprinkle with cinnamon and serve cold. Store in refrigerator.

Per Wheel: Calories: 331, Protein: 7 gm., Fat: 15 gm., Carbohydrates: 42 gm.

Orange Yogurt Cake with Syrup
Yaourtopitta me Syropi
Serves 16

Sift together farina, flour, baking powder and baking soda into a large mixing bowl. Add 1½ cups honey, the yogurt, almonds (if used) and orange juice concentrate. Stir until mixture is well combined. Pour the batter into a well-greased 9" x 13" baking pan and bake in a preheated 350° oven until top is a light chestnut color, about 45 minutes.

While the cake is baking, make a syrup by combining honey, water and orange slice in a saucepan and bring to a boil. Lower the heat and simmer for 5 minutes. Skim off the froth and remove the orange slice. As soon as you remove the cake from the oven, pour the hot syrup over it. Do not cut the cake until all syrup is absorbed and cake has cooled.

Per Serving: Calories: 343, Protein: 2 gm., Fat: 1 gm.,
*   Carbohydrates: 87gm.*

3 cups farina

½ cup flour

2 tsps. baking powder

1 tsp. baking soda

1½ cups honey

2 cups yogurt

½ cup almonds, blanched and coarsely chopped (opt.)

2 Tbsps. frozen orange juice concentrate

SYRUP
3 cups honey
2½ cups water
1 thin slice of orange

Yogurt Cake

Yaourtopitta

Serves 16

½ cup butter

⅔ cups honey
  or ¾ sugar

3 eggs
  or egg substitute

1 cup yogurt

1 tsp. grated lemon
  peel

1 tsp. vanilla

1 tsp. cinnamon

2½ cups flour

2 tsps. baking soda

pinch of salt

1 cup almonds,
  blanched and
  chopped

Cream together butter and sugar or honey in a medium mixing bowl. Add eggs or egg substitute and beat until fluffy. Add yogurt, lemon peel, vanilla and cinnamon. Sift flour with baking powder, baking soda and salt. Add to the creamed mixture and blend well. Fold in almonds.

Pour into a greased 9" x 13" baking pan and bake in a preheated 350° oven until top is a light chestnut color, about 30 minutes. Let cool on a rack, then remove from pan. Cut in squares.

Per Serving: Calories: 230, Protein: 5 gm., Fat: 6 gm., Carbohydrates: 26 gm.

Lemonade
Lemonada

Serves 6

Lemonade is a delicious and popular beverage for refreshing one's guests in Greece on a hot summer's day.

In a pitcher, combine lemon juice, sugar or honey and water. Stir until sugar or honey is dissolved.

Serve in chilled glasses with a slice of lemon or mint.

1 cup lemon juice

2 cups sugar or honey (less if you prefer it more tart)

6 cups ice water

Per Serving: Calories: 256, Protein: 0 gm., Fat: 0 gm., Carbohydrates: 67 gm.

Measures & Equivalents

US Standard Measures	Approximate Metric Equivalents
3 teaspoons = 1 tablespoon	1 ounce = 28 gm.
4 tablespoons = ¼ cup	1 pound = 454 gm.
5⅓ tablespoons = ⅓ cup	1 teaspoon = 5 ml.
16 tablespoons = 1 cup	1 tablespoon = 15 ml.
1 cup = 8 fluid ounces	1 fluid ounce = 30 ml.
4 cups = 1 quart	1 cup = 240 ml.
4 quarts = 1 gallon	1 quart = 950 ml.
	1 gallon = 3.8 l.

Index

BOOK PUBLISHING COMPANY

since 1974—books that educate, inspire, and empower

To find your favorite vegetarian and soyfood products online,
visit: www.healthy-eating.com

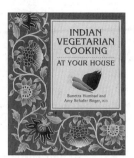

Indian Vegetarian
Cooking at Your House
Sunetra Humbad &
Amy Schafer Boger, MD
978-1-57067-004-6
$12.95

Nonna's Italian Kitchen
Bryanna Clark Grogan
978-1-57067-055-8
$14.95

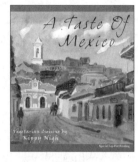

A Taste of Mexico
Kippy Nigh
978-1-57067-028-2
$14.95

Olive Oil Cookery
Maher A. Abbas, MD &
Marilyn Spiegl
978-0-913990-11-7
$12.95

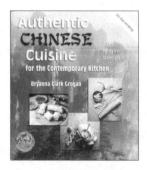

Authentic Chinese Cuisine
Bryanna Clark Grogan
978-1-57067-101-2
$12.95

From the Tables of Lebanon
Dalal Holmin & Maher Abbas, MD
978-1-57067-040-4
$12.95

Purchase these health titles and cookbooks from your local bookstore or
natural food store, or you can buy them directly from:

Book Publishing Company • P.O. Box 99 • Summertown, TN 38483   1-800-695-2241

Please include $3.95 per book for shipping and handling.